D1498284

Brassey's *Modern Military Equipment*

TANKS

MAIN BATTLE TANKS AND LIGHT TANKS

Marsh Gelbart

First English Edition 1996

UK editorial offices: Brassey's, 33 John Street, London WC1N 2AT
UK orders: Marston Book Services, PO Box 269, Abingdon, OX14 4SD

North American orders: Brassey's Inc., PO Box 960,
Herndon, VA 22070, USA

Marsh Gelbart has asserted his moral right to be identified as
the author of this work.

Library of Congress Cataloging in Publication Data available

British Library Cataloguing in Publication Data
A catalogue record for this book is available from the British Library

ISBN 1 85753 168 X Hardcover

Typeset by Images Book Production Ltd
Printed by Bookcraft Ltd, Midsomer Norton, Somerset

CONTENTS

This book is aimed at those with an interest in armoured vehicles, from the enthusiast to the squaddie: those who read about armour and those who man it. Although it gives a reasonably thorough commentary on contemporary main battle tanks (MBTs) and light tanks, it is not all encompassing. The book is not intended as the gold standard reference work on armoured vehicles, nor as a tank spotter's bible. Limits on space preclude that. The many armoured engineering and recovery vehicles built upon tank hulls will be examined in a separate work.

However I hope that this book will give the reader some insight into why tanks from different manufacturers have different characteristics. Subtle shifts in emphasis from one manufacturer to the next can lead to the construction of very different fighting machines. The different design philosophies of the major or the most innovative producers – China, France, Germany, Israel, Russia, Sweden, UK and the USA – will be surveyed very briefly.

THE IRON TRINITY

Tanks have measurable characteristics that give some indication of a vehicle's fighting potential. The three basic characteristics – the Iron Trinity of tank design – are: protection, firepower and mobility. Most designers attempt to put the largest calibre weapon practicable on their MBTs. However the situation is not as clear cut for protection and mobility; these two attributes are to some extent competitive. An increase in armour protection is bought at the expense of additional weight; extra weight places a strain on the tank's engine and reduces agility. The trick of successful tank design is to blend these features to produce an effective fighting machine.

PROTECTION

The mechanics of protecting a tank used to be easy. A tank's armour, of homogeneous steel plate, merely needed to be as thick as possible. Wherever feasible armour was sloped, which increased equivalent thickness and maximised ballistic protection. This solution worked to a greater or lesser extent against kinetic energy attacks – that is, against projectiles that rely on their velocity to kill a tank.

Kinetic energy projectiles are fired from high pressure cannon, usually mounted on armoured vehicles. In essence, a kinetic energy round depends on its speed and mass to pierce a target. The narrower the cross-section of a projectile – with a given velocity and mass – the greater its penetrative qualities. Modern armour piercing penetrators are arrow-like, with a length-to-diameter ratio of approximately 20:1. The denser the material of the penetrator, the better. Tungsten and depleted uranium are the materials of choice at time of writing. The penetrators are enclosed by plastic sabots, which are stripped off the penetrators when the projectile leaves the cannon. This type of shell is referred to as an armoured piercing discarding sabot, or APDS. Recently there has been the development of a more lethal projectile, the armoured piercing fin stabilised discarding sabot (APFSDS).

Tanks face the additional threat of projectiles that rely on chemical energy – primarily High Explosive Anti-Tank (HEAT) warheads. HEAT warheads are able to cut through the thickest of conventional armour, irrespective of their speed. A shaped charge releases a cutting jet of molten copper and gas that can pierce a tank. They can be fired by infantry anti-tank weapons, as well as from tank cannon.

Early attempts at defeating HEAT warheads relied upon stand-off or spaced armour. The first employs simple appliqué armour, often of sheet steel, to detonate HEAT warheads prematurely before they pierce the armour shell proper. The latter consists of a protective shell made up of separate layers of armour with gaps between them. Spaced armour often incorporates diesel fuel cells between the inner and outer layers, which help to degrade the effect of HEAT projectiles.

Stand-off armour is not particularly effective against modern kinetic projectiles. However, spaced armour is effective against kinetic energy attack if manufactured of modern composites. More advanced armour arrays incorporate ceramics and metal alloys in a laminate or matrix. Such defences – the most famous of which is the British-designed Chobham – offer greatly increased protection against both HEAT and kinetic shells. The **5** problem with modern compound armours is that they are complex and difficult to shape; ideally they need to be incorporated in a tank's design from its inception. Depleted uranium armour plating has similar restrictions, plus the unavoidable fact that it is very heavy.

A new design trend is to have a portion of a tank's protective shell made of removable armour modules. These modules are attached to the steel skeleton of a tank, and can be replaced if battle damaged or when new more advanced composites become available.

When the Israelis invaded southern Lebanon in 1982, their tanks carried a new type of armour that offered greatly increased protection against HEAT charges. Small tiles of reactive armour were fitted over the tanks' vulnerable points. The reactive armour, known as Blazer, consisted of a layer of insensitive explosive sandwiched between two metal plates. Blazer tiles do not react if hit by small arms fire. However if hit by a HEAT projectile, reactive armour explodes, disrupting the cutting jet formed by HEAT warheads and reducing their penetrative effect by up to 75%. Blazer and similar armour on the market is fairly cheap and easy to retrofit; its major failing is that has limited effectiveness against kinetic energy weapons.

Reactive armour has limited the effectiveness of simple HEAT shells. However, new generations of HEAT projectiles with tandem warheads are in development – the first charge intended to blast away reactive armour. Another type of projectile is sometimes encountered. Known as High explosive Squash Head (HESH), this shell is thin walled and contains plastic explosive. On contact with the target, the plastic explosive detonates. The shock waves tear off a high speed scab from the inner layer of armour, which cuts through men and machinery inside the tank's fighting compartment.

Other defensive systems include automatic fire detection/suppression equipment. In addition, modern tanks employ explosion detectors and halon gas dispensers. NBC systems are also fitted to most battle tanks, as are smoke grenade dischargers.

In the future tanks are likely to carry active armour systems. These will consist of sensors and launch pods for assorted mini-projectiles. These will be able not just to warn if a tank is being painted by a targeting laser, but to detect incoming rounds and respond by launching mini projectiles to destroy or decoy them. The Russian

Shtora-1 electro-optical active defence suite indicates impending developments. Tanks, like aircraft, are becoming weapons platforms, in which electronic offensive and defensive systems are becoming more important.

FIREPOWER

Firepower and protection have been locked in an ascending competitive spiral ever since the early days of tank warfare. There has been a gradual increase in gun calibre since 1945. The British 105mm rifled cannon, ubiquitous in the 1960s and 1970s, has been supplanted by a German designed 120mm smoothbore weapon on modern Western tanks. MBTs from the old Soviet bloc have standardised on a 125mm smoothbore weapon. Russian tanks have recently acquired the capability to fire specially developed anti-tank missiles from their cannon, if appropriate fire control is fitted.

One of the major changes in armoured vehicles in recent years has been the arrival of autoloaders. Autoloaders were pioneered (initially with dubious results) by the Soviet Union. Autoloaders are now found on the French Leclerc MBT and are being trialled by several major manufacturers. An autoloader allows the reduction of a tank's crew from four to three. This allows the development of more compact tanks.

MOBILITY

Mobility is an elusive concept to quantify. At first glance the tank with a high power-to-weight ratio is going to be more mobile than a heavier vehicle with a less impressive ratio. However under combat conditions, the heavier machine may be able to waddle over the battlefield and survive hits that would destroy or disable the lighter tank. In effect the heavier tank has better battlefield manoeuvrability than the more agile competitor. There is a constant interaction between the relative priority given to mobility and protection.

As well as tactical mobility, a tank's strategic mobility needs to be taken into consideration. Can the machine be transported by rail or by aircraft? Is it too heavy to cross river bridges in its expected area of operation?

Since World War Two there has been a sustained growth in the power of engines and the sophistication of transmission and running gear. Petrol engines have been superseded by diesel, as the latter give longer range and are less prone to the risk of fire and explosion. Automatic transmissions have become the norm in newer tanks to reduce the driver's workload.

Present efforts concentrate on increasing power output whilst keeping the physical size of the engine as small as possible. Turbine engines, with their compact mass and great power, may represent the future. However turbines in service at present have higher fuel demands than diesel engines; they have not been adopted by many manufacturers. Soviet, Russian and Chinese tanks have less internal fuel storage space than Western tanks. A deliberate choice was made to use jettisonable, external fuel tanks as the norm, to keep the size of their tanks to a minimum.

Torsion bar suspension systems remain the most common in use. Britain and Israel have used variations of the Horstman suspension system, as they are easier to repair after mine damage, and offer some ballistic protection to the hull. Latest trends in suspension design have concentrated on hydropneumatic suspension systems. These offer an increased range of movement for individual road wheels, and give a more cushioned ride. Better shock absorption allows tanks to use their engines' full power, without shaking crew and equipment to bits whilst crossing rough terrain.

FIRE CONTROL

If gun calibre and ammunition are responsible for destructive power, then fire control is accountable for accuracy and speed. Basic optics and rangefinding machine guns have been superseded by sophisticated day/night sights integrated with laser rangefinders. Environmental sensors, fully stabilised cannon and digital ballistic computers have taken the guesswork out of computations. The latest fire control systems use 'Hunter Killer' systems, where the commander and gunner both have independent sights and controls and are both capable of acquiring and engaging a target. A commander can spot and automatically lock on to a target, then hand it over to his gunner to engage, as the commander searches for his next victim.

More often than not the first shot is a kill. Given this, acquisition of the enemy and improved, electronically enhanced situational awareness is vital. Situational awareness is the ability of tank crew to survey the environment and be aware of tactical developments and approaching threats. As electronics and optics become more sophisticated, the tank crew are more aware of what is happening around them. Future developments will allow individual tanks to electronically transmit much more tactical data, including visual information, to one another.

Despite all the sophistication, it is worth remembering that the best way to get a decent view of events is for the commander to stick his head out of the turret. This is risky but battle proven. If all the complex electronics and optics are down, then the commander still needs to be able to fight the tank using the ever reliable Mk 1 eyeball.

MEASURING THE BEAST

A tank's configuration can have a considerable bearing both on crew survival and on battlefield signature. The conventional tank has its powerpack and drive sprocket at the rear. There are a few exceptions – the Israeli Merkava being the most prominent – where tanks have the powerpack and drive sprocket at the front. There are clear advantages to the front engined layout. The prime advantage is that the mass of the engine helps to protect the crew from projectiles that pierce the tank's shell. The frontal arc of any tank, along with its turret, is the section of the vehicle most likely to take hits. If the Merkava's armour is penetrated over its frontal arc, then it will probably suffer a mobility kill, but its crew is more likely to survive than in the case of a conventional tank. A front mounted engine also allows the installation of a door at the tank's rear. This allows a crew to bail out under armour rather than have to endure an exposed scramble out of the turret. The additional space at the back of the Merkava allows stowage of extra ammunition, or even the transport of a handful of infantrymen over a short distance. The layout's major disadvantage is that a front engined tank cannot depress its cannon quite as much as a conventional tank. The Merkava probably cannot depress its gun beyond minus 8 degrees.

Tanks originating in the ex-Soviet Union are more compact and low slung than those from the West, and on the face of it have a smaller battlefield signature. However there is a difference between a tank's overall height, and its tactical height. The latter can be defined as the portion of a tank that has to be exposed to the enemy before it can bring its gun to bear. Western tanks, in general, are designed to depress their guns about minus 10 degrees. Russian, Chinese and Eastern European tanks are only able to depress their cannon about minus 5 degrees. Tanks that can depress their guns by a greater amount, find it easier to fire from a hull down position. They effectively have a lower tactical height, than a low slung tank that has to expose more of its turret and hull to bring its gun to bear. This design flaw has been a major handicap of Russian post-war tank design.

Other important facets of tank design need careful consideration.

Firstly, ergonomics. If a tank has poor human engineering and is cramped and uncomfortable, then the crew will have difficulty in fighting the machine to its maximum potential.

Secondly, sustainability. If a tank has good endurance, as a result of low fuel consumption and/or generous fuel capacity it has sustainability. Likewise if it has ammunition stowage capacity above average, then it can continue to fight for longer.

Thirdly, availability. If a tank uses well-proven components and does not use too much unfamiliar technology, then it will be easier to maintain and be more available for combat.

Fourthly, battlefield signature. Efforts need to be made to reduce the visual, thermal, electromagnetic and noise signature of any fighting vehicle. Avoiding detection is the best way to improve chances of survival, particularly in the case of light tanks which have to rely on stealth rather than armour. Tall soldiers live short lives!

CONCLUSION

Tanks remain one of the dominant weapon systems found on the battlefield, despite premature declarations of their obsolescence. For the foreseeable future, as long as tanks are used in combination with other arms, they will maintain their importance.

One final word. It is worth remembering that history is replete with examples of armies defeating opponents equipped with more sophisticated weaponry. It is not just the technology of an individual tank that counts. An army needs to have developed an armoured warfare doctrine suitable for local conditions, and to have trained hard to realise it. Most importantly an army must be able to integrate armour, artillery, mechanised infantry and air power into a coherent whole. Those unable to fight a Combined Arms War effectively, are likely to be amongst the losers, no matter how technically sophisticated their MBTs may be.

MANUFACTURER: TAMSE

BACKGROUND

At Argentina's request, the German company Thyssen Henschel designed a medium tank for Argentina's armed forces. Once the first few prototypes were delivered by the German firm, the Argentineans started production, albeit a production run destined to be disrupted by financial upheaval.

The TAM (Tanque Argentino Mediano) was based upon the strengthened hull of the German, Marder infantry fighting vehicle, (IFV). The turret, weapon and associated systems are of new design.

PROTECTION

The vehicle only has the protection of a heavy IFV rather than of an MBT. The hull is made out of all-welded steel and has a good ballistic shape to enhance protection. The TAM's frontal arc has protection sufficient to keep out 40mm cannon shells. The engine being mounted at the front, adds its bulk to protect the crew compartment.

FIREPOWER

The original German built prototypes were fitted with a Rheinmetall 105mm rifled cannon. A similar Argentinean weapon has been fitted to production vehicles. The weapon has a thermal shroud and is stabilised on two axes. It fires standard NATO ammunition. The fire-control system is effective but basic, consisting of a coincidence rangefinder.

MOBILITY

Prototypes were fitted with the same front-mounted engine as mounted on the Marder, however the production models are fitted with a supercharged version of the original powerpack. A torsion bar suspension system is fitted.

ASSESSMENT

The tank is a credible attempt to produce a light tank for low threat environments, reconnaissance and internal security missions. Firepower and mobility are good. Some of the on-board equipment is beginning to look a little dated. The German company Thyssen Henschel

TAM medium tank.   *(Courtesy of Manufacturer)*

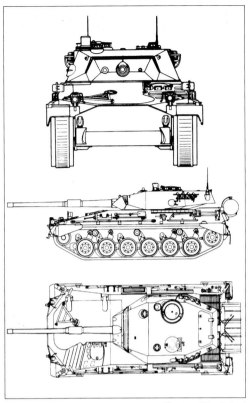

Prototype:	1976
In service:	1979
Crew:	4
Armament:	Main
Combat weight:	30,000kg
Power-to-weight ratio:	24hp/t
Ground pressure:	0.78kg/cm²
Length gun forward:	8.23m
Hull length:	6.75m
Hull width:	3.29m
Height	
(to commands cupola):	2.66m
Ground clearance:	0.45m
Power pack:	MTU MB 833 Ka-500 V-6 turbo-charged diesel of 720hp/t coupled to an automatic transmission
Max road speed:	75km/h
Max range (internal fuel):	590 km
Fording (unprepared):	1.5m
Gradient:	60%
Side slope:	30%
Vertical obstacle:	1.0m

(Courtesy of Manufacturer)

offers an improved variant known as the TH 301. This offers a more powerful engine, a modern fire control and targeting system, and is fitted with the Rheinmetall 105mm rifled cannon.

The TAM was intended to have a production run of 512 vehicles including an IFV variant. In fact only 400 vehicles were produced, a proportion of which went directly into storage. Some hulls may be converted into self-propelled artillery vehicles or multiple rocket launchers.

SERVICE STATUS
Argentina has approximately 200 in service.

MANUFACTURER: BERNARDINI S/A

BACKGROUND

The Brazilian Army requires a more capable replacement for its M41 light tanks. In 1984 Bernardini demonstrated the MB-3 Tamoya, which it hoped would gain a production order. Initial prototypes of the MB-3 Tamoya were rather basic fighting machines, but by 1987 the more capable Tamoyo III was being trialled. As of 1996 no production order had been placed. The fact that the Brazilian Army intends to purchase 61 Leopard 1 as a stop-gap, may raise some doubts as to the Tamoyo's future.

PROTECTION

The MB-3 Tamoyo has a well-shaped welded steel hull and turret. Spaced armour, possibly incorporating some laminated material, is used. The Tamoyo III has more extensive protection using more advanced composite armour. Both variants carry smoke grenades to screen their movements, and an NBC system as standard.

FIREPOWER

The MB-3 Tamoyo is fitted with an ENGESA built version of the Belgium 90mm Cockerill rifled cannon, and carries 68 rounds for the weapon. Fire control incorporates day/night sights and a laser rangefinder. The Tamoyo III mounts the more capable British 105mm rifled cannon. Of 50 rounds of 105mm ammunition, 18 are in the turret.

MOBILITY

The original MB-3 Tamoyo is distinctly under-powered, using a 500hp diesel. The Tamoyo III uses a more robust 736hp powerpack. This engine is an option that can be fitted to the earlier Tamoyo variant. Both tanks have the same torsion bar suspension, the Tamoyo III a more modern transmission.

ASSESSMENT

The tanks, in particular the Tamoyo III, are capable if basic fighting machines. They match local requirements but are not premier MBTS. Some doubt hangs over the tanks future production on a large scale.

MB-3 Tamoyo.   *(Courtesy of Manufacturer)*

SERVICE STATUS

Not yet in production. Several hundred tanks of the Tamoyo's class are wanted by the Brazilian military.

Prototype:	1984, MB-3 Tamoyo. 1987, Tamoyo III
In service:	Not yet in production
Crew:	4
Armament:	Main, 90mm rifled cannon – MB-3 Tamoyo. 105mm rifled cannon – Tamoyo III. Secondary, coaxial 1 x 12.7mm MG, anti-aircraft 1 x 7.62mm MG
Combat weight:	30,000kg – MB-3 Tamoyo, 31,000kg – Tamoyo III
Power-to-weight ratio:	16.6hp/t MB-3 Tamoyo. 23.74hp/t Tamoyo III
Ground pressure:	0.72kg/cm^2
Length gun forward:	8.77m – MB-3 Tamoyo, 8.9m Tamoyo III
Hull length:	6.5m
Hull width:	3.2m
Height (to commander's cupola):	2.5m – MB-3 Tamoyo, 2.65m - Tamoyo III
Ground clearance:	0.5m
Power pack:	Saab Scania DSI-14 diesel of 500hp coupled to an Allison Cd-500 transmission, or as on Tamoyo III an optional Detroit Diesel 8V-92TA of 736hp
Max road speed:	67km/h
Max range (internal fuel):	550 km
Fording (Unprepared):	1.3m
Gradient:	60%
Side slope:	30%
Vertical obstacle:	0.71m

Different views of MB-3 Tamoya. (above: *Courtesy of Manufacturer*)

MANUFACTURER: ENGESA SA

BACKGROUND

The Osorio is an advanced tank designed by Brazilian industry, but with many major components supplied by British manufacturers. The conceptional development of the tank dates back to 1982 and its first prototype appeared in 1985. The tank was intended to fulfil a Brazilian army requirement for a new MBT and was seriously considered by Saudi Arabia for licence built production. Orders by the Brazilian military for Leopard 1 MBTs and by Saudi Arabia for the Abrams, have placed the future of the Osorio under severe threat.

PROTECTION

The manufacturer has developed a new variant of passive, composite armour to defend the Osorio against attack. The bi-metal shell of the Osorio is coupled with a passive laminate for increased protection. Ballistic shaping is good, wherever possible sloped armour is used to advantage on both hull and turret.

The tank has an automatic fire detection/suppression system for its crew compartment and separate equipment for the engine compartment.

NBC kit can be fitted according to customer requirements.

FIREPOWER

Two distinct turret options are on offer to prospective purchasers. Version 1 mounts the British L7 105mm rifled cannon, Version 2 carries the French 120mm smoothbore gun built by GIAT. Both turrets were supplied by Vickers Defence Systems. Both turrets are designed to stow 12 rounds. The 105mm version of the tank carries 45 rounds for the main armament; the 120mm variant has storage space for 38 rounds. Blow off vents are designed to direct any explosion away from the crew compartment should the ammunition brew up.

Fire control is modern and comprehensive, with two levels of sophistication on offer. The first integrates a laser rangefinder with the gunner's and commander's day/night sights. The commander is able to override the gunner's controls. The more sophisticated alternative is built by Marconi and incorporates a laser rangefinder with stabilised gunner's and commander's periscopes with independent thermal imaging for both gunner and commander. Both fire control systems have extensive meteorological and environmental inputs.

Osorio approaching the camera at speed.   *(Courtesy of John Norris)*

MOBILITY

A powerful diesel engine and automatic transmission give a high power to weight ratio. The tank has a modern hydropneumatic suspension system developed by Dunlop which gives the Osorio a good cross-country performance.

ASSESSMENT

The Osorio is a very advanced project for Brazilian industry to undertake. The manufacturers purchased some of the best components available from abroad to produce a potentially formidable tank. Firepower and mobility in particular are first class. At time of writing it appears that the Osorio may never be put into production, not through any failing of the design but because of political and economic circumstances.

SERVICE STATUS

Not yet in production or service.

Prototype:	1985
In service:	Not yet in service
Crew:	4
Armament:	Main, 105mm rifled cannon or 120mm smoothbore cannon. Secondary, coaxial 1 x 7.62mm MG, anti-aircraft 1 x 7.62mm MG
Combat weight:	40,900kg, 105mm armed Version 1. 43,700kg 120mm armed Version 2
Power-to-weight ratio:	26.89hp/t Version 1. 25.17hp/t Version 2
Ground pressure:	0.72kg/cm^2 Version 1. 0.85kg/cm^2 Version 2
Length gun forward:	9.36m Version 1. 10.1m Version 2
Hull length:	7.13m
Hull width:	3.26m
Height (to commander's cupola):	2.68m Version 1. 2.89m Version 2
Ground clearance:	0.46m
Power pack:	Deutz MWM TBD234 turbocharged diesel of 1,100hp coupled to an automatic transmission
Max road speed:	70km/h
Max range:	550 km
Fording (unprepared):	1.2m
Gradient:	60%
Side slope:	30%
Vertical obstacle:	1.15m

China has been one of the more prolific of the world's post war tank producers. The core of China's tank design has not been particularly innovative; it has copied obsolescent Soviet designs. There has been a process of adaptation as the Chinese have tailored ex-Soviet design to suit local conditions. Chinese tanks, as their Soviet predecessors, have been adversely affected by their inability to depress their main armament below an angle of -5 degrees. In general the design of Chinese tanks has been evolutionary, with improvements introduced gradually over a period of time. Although basically simple, Chinese tanks have proven popular among developing countries as they are cheap to purchase and easy to operate.

In recent years, the technological capability of Chinese tank manufacturers has increased. They have grafted components purchased from abroad onto indigenously designed fighting vehicles to produce more effective tanks. It is reasonable to suppose that as China's manufacturers improve, their tank designs will become more sophisticated and the machines more potent on the battlefield.

MANUFACTURER: CHINESE STATE ORDNANCE
FACTORIES

BACKGROUND

The Type 59 is based on the old Soviet T-54 tank
supplied to China in the early 1950s. Although obsolete,
the tank has undergone successive modifications that
have improved its fighting qualities. The most notable
of these modifications were the fitting of a 105mm
cannon similar to the British L7, and better fire control
systems. The tank was constructed between 1956 and
the middle 1980s.

PROTECTION

The tank has the same thick armour as the T-55, and
the turret the same excellent ballistic shape. However
ammunition is stowed in the turret, meaning that if the
armoured shell was pierced, then there is the likelihood
of catastrophic secondary explosions.

The Type 59 Retrofit Package introduced
by China in 1986 offered an NBC protection system.

FIREPOWER

The Type 59 originally mounted a 100mm cannon. The
Type 59-II variant carried a 105mm gun, possibly Israeli
in origin, whilst Royal Ordnance offers an upgrade of
the Type 59 with the British L7 cannon.

The Type 59-I was fitted with an infra-red searchlight
and in the 1980s with a laser rangefinder. The Type
59-II had an improved fire control system and a stabilised main armament. The Type 59 Retrofit Package
offered a new Chinese designed tungsten APFSDS
round as well as an upgraded gun stabilisation and fire
control.

MOBILITY

The powerpack, power to weight ratio and overall
mobility are those of the T-54. The Type 59 Retrofit
Package proposed a 730hp diesel which considerably
enhanced speed, acceleration and mobility.

ASSESSMENT

A simple, rather crude fighting vehicle that has limited
effectiveness on the modern battlefield. The various

Type 59 retrofitted with a 105 mm cannon.

(Courtesy of Tank Museum)

upgrades did increase the Type 59's fighting abilities and extended its useful life.

SERVICE STATUS

In service with Albania 15 tanks, plus others non-operational. Bangladesh, 20. China, approximately 6,000 some upgraded. Congo, 15. Iran, 229. Iraq, number unknown. Korea, (North), 175. Pakistan, 1,200 some upgraded. Tanzania 30, many non-operational. Vietnam 350. Zimbabwe 40.

Prototype:	1956
In service:	1957
Crew:	4
Armament:	Main 100mm rifled cannon. Type 59-II has a 105mm rifled cannon. Secondary, 1 x 7.62mm MG, bow 1 x 7.62mm MG, anti-aircraft 1 x 12.7mm MG
Combat weight:	36,000kg
Power-to-weight ratio:	14.44hp/t
Ground pressure:	0.8kg/cm^2
Length gun forward:	9m
Hull length:	6.04m
Hull width:	3.27m
Height:	2.59m
Ground clearance:	0.43m
Power pack:	Model 12150L V-12 liquid cooled diesel of 520hp coupled to a manual transmission
Max road speed:	50km/h
Max range (internal fuel):	420 km
Fording (unprepared):	1.4m
Gradient:	60%
Side slope:	40%
Vertical obstacle:	0.8m

MANUFACTURER: CHINESE STATE ORDNANCE FACTORIES

BACKGROUND

Natural outgrowths of the Type 59 MBT, the Type 69 and Type 79 tanks attempted to integrate further advances in fire control systems and night vision equipment to the basic hull design of the Type 59. Demand for these tanks was generated by the Iran/Iraq war. The tank being simple, relatively easy to operate and available, sold well to both sides in that war. Production of the Type 69 and Type 79 is now probably complete.

PROTECTION

The protection level of the Type 69 and Type 79 tanks remains that of the T-55 with all the advantages and qualifications that entails. Ammunition stowage is vulnerable, a catastrophic explosion likely if the tank's shell is pierced. Some efforts have been made to increase protection. Iraqi Type 69 tanks encountered in the Gulf War had appliqué armour fitted to their turrets. The Type 69-II and Type 79 were both given side skirts

to protect their running gear.

The Type 69 and Type 79 both have NBC protection systems and fire detection/suppression systems.

FIREPOWER

An initial attempt to mount a 100mm smoothbore cannon on the Type 69 tank proved unsatisfactory. The Type 69-I, a Type 69 with an externally mounted laser range finder, also carried the smoothbore weapon. After a small number of tanks carrying the smoothbore cannon were built, production shifted to the Type 69-II which carries the customary rifled 100mm cannon. The Type 69-I was equipped with infra-red sights and night fighting equipment. The Type 69-II has a better fire control system and an externally mounted laser range finder.

The Type 79 tank is a further development of the basic Type 59/Type 69 tanks. It carries a 105mm rifled cannon with a thermal shroud, an internal laser range finder and a fire control ballistic computer.

MOBILITY

The Type 69-II has an upgraded powerpack when compared to the Type 59 complete with hydraulic

Type 69-II tank.

(Courtesy of Tank Museum)

assistance for steering and clutch. The tank also has double pin rubber tracks. Suspension is torsion bar.

It is unclear if the Type 79 has been fitted with a more powerful 780hp powerpack.

ASSESSMENT
These tanks are basic fighting vehicles adequate for armies facing low technology threats. They are perfectly serviceable fighting vehicles but not top notch MBTs.

SERVICE STATUS
The Type 69 is in service with China, some 200 tanks. Iran, 220. Iraq, number unknown. Pakistan, 200, (where the tank is assembled under licence). Thailand, 50 tanks in store. The Type 79 is in service with China in small numbers.

Type 69

Prototype:	1968
In service:	1969
Crew:	4
Armament:	Main, 100mm rifled cannon. Secondary, coaxial 1 x 7.62mm MG, bow 1 x 7.62mm MG, anti-aircraft 1 x 7.62mm MG
Combat weight:	Type 69-I, 36500kg. Type 69-II 36,700kg
Power-to-weight ratio:	15.89hp/t, Type 69-I. 15.80 Type 69-II
Ground pressure:	0.82-0.83kg/cm^2
Length gun forward:	8.66m
Hull length:	6.24m
Hull width:	3.3m
Height (with AA gun):	2.87m
Ground clearance:	0.43m
Power pack:	Type 12150L V-12 liquid cooled diesel of 580hp coupled to a manual transmission
Max road speed:	50 km
Max range (internal fuel):	420 km
Fording (unprepared):	1.4m
Gradient:	60%
Side slope:	40%
Vertical obstacle:	0.8m

MANUFACTURER: CHINESE STATE ORDNANCE FACTORIES

BACKGROUND
This tank was representative of an interim stage of Chinese tank design. It borrowed heavily from the legacy of the Type 59, but began to introduce new characteristics to Chinese MBT development. The tank was not produced in great numbers and was really a stepping stone towards creating more advanced models.

PROTECTION
The level of protection is the same as the Type 69 and its successors. The only marked difference is that optional plates of composite armour can be fitted to the glacis and turret. The tank also has a turret basket that extends along the sides and rear of the turret. As well as offering storage space, the basket has a secondary function, it helps to detonate HEAT charges before they impact on the turret proper. The tank has side skirts to protect its running gear against HEAT projectiles.

The tank has NBC protection and an automatic fire detection/suppression system. It has smoke grenade launchers and is also able to make smoke by injecting a fuel aerosol into its exhaust.

FIREPOWER
The Type 80 has an improved fire control system with a better ballistic computer, a range finder integrated into stabilised sights, and a stabilised main cannon. The tank has better passive night vision equipment than its predecessors. A stationary Type 80 can engage moving targets with its 105mm rifled cannon. A variant known as the Type 80-II has superior gun stabilisation and laying.

MOBILITY
The Type 80 is fitted with a new, more powerful, engine. This gives a superior power to weight ratio than previous Chinese tanks and results in better mobility. The tank has a new torsion bar suspension with six rubber-tyred road wheels each side. Four wheels on each side are equipped with hydraulic shock absorbers.

The Type 80-II may have an automatic transmission.

Type 80 MBT.   *(Courtesy of Lt Col Flach)*

ASSESSMENT

The tank still has elements of its Type 59 heritage and is a basic design but demonstrates the potential of future Chinese tanks. Production has probably stopped, supplanted by newer models.

SERVICE STATUS

Small numbers in service with the Chinese armed forces.

Prototype:	1985
In service:	1988
Crew:	4
Armament:	Main, 105mm rifled cannon. Secondary, coaxial 1 x 7.62mm MG, anti-aircraft 1 x 12.7mm MG
Combat weight:	38,000kg
Power-to-weight ratio:	19.2hp/t
Ground pressure:	n/a
Length gun forward:	9.33m
Hull length:	6.325m
Hull width:	3.37m
Height (to turret roof):	2.29m
Ground clearance:	0.48m
Power pack:	V-12 diesel of 730hp coupled to a manual transmission
Max road speed:	60km/h
Max range (internal fuel):	430 km
Fording (unprepared):	1.4m
Gradient:	60%
Side slope:	40%
Vertical obstacle:	0.8m

MANUFACTURER: CHINESE STATE ORDNANCE FACTORIES

BACKGROUND

Announced in 1989, the Type 85-II owes more to its immediate predecessor than to obsolete Soviet tanks. The Type 85-II and its variants reflect the increased sophistication of Chinese tank design. The initial version of the Type 85-II carried a 105mm cannon, the later Type 85-IIM model, announced in 1992, is fitted with a 125mm smoothbore cannon and an autoloader.

PROTECTION

For the first time in Chinese tank construction, the Type 85 has a welded rather than a cast turret. This employs composite armour to increase protection; composite armour is also incorporated in the hull.

The tank has smoke grenades as standard and an NBC protection system.

FIREPOWER

The Type 85-II has a 105mm rifled cannon and a four man crew. The Type 85-IIM has a more potent smoothbore 125mm weapon and as an autoloader has been fitted a three-man crew. Both tanks have their weapons covered with a thermal shroud. The Type 85-II and Type 85-IIM both have fully stabilised main armament. For the first time in a Chinese tank, the gunner can engage a moving target whilst his tank itself is on the move. The cannon has a maximum angle of depression of minus 6 degrees, better than most Soviet designed tanks, but still not as useful as the minus 10 degree norm of Western tanks. The gunner, driver and commander all are equipped with second generation image intensification night vision sights.

MOBILITY

The tank appears to have the same supercharged diesel powerpack as the Type 80; because of its greater weight the Type 85-IIM has a lower power to weight ratio. Suspension is torsion bar; tracks are all steel.

ASSESSMENT

More than just a rebuild of elderly Soviet designs, the Type 85-IIM demonstrates a noteworthy advance in capabilities by Chinese industry.

SERVICE STATUS

In service, in relatively small numbers, with China and Pakistan.

(Type 85-IIM)

Prototype:	1986
In service:	1992
Crew:	3
Armament:	Main, 125mm smoothbore cannon. Secondary, coaxial 1 x 7.62mm MG, anti-aircraft 1 x 12.7mm MG
Combat weight:	41,000kg
Power-to-weight ratio:	18.5hp/t
Ground pressure:	Not available
Length gun forward:	10.28m
Hull length:	Not available
Hull width:	3.45m
Height (to turret top):	2.30m
Ground clearance:	0.48m
Power pack:	V-12 supercharged diesel of 730hp coupled to a semi-automatic transmission
Max road speed:	57km/h
Max range (internal fuel):	430 km, (estimate)
Fording (unprepared):	1.4m
Gradient:	60%
Side slope:	40%
Vertical obstacle:	0.8m

MANUFACTURER: CHINESE STATE ORDNANCE FACTORIES

BACKGROUND

A further evolution of the Type 85-IIM with improvements concentrating on protection and mobility. The tank was announced in 1995.

PROTECTION

The tank has had composite armour incorporated in its design from the beginning. Modular composite armour on the turret can be removed and replaced either if damaged or if better armour laminates become available. The special armour applied to the tank hull is not removable.

The tank is equipped with smoke grenade dischargers; it also has the ability to lay smoke by injecting a fuel aerosol into the engine exhaust. A fire detection/suppression system and a collective NBC system are standard.

FIREPOWER

The tank carries the same 125mm smoothbore gun as the Type 85-IIM. It also uses a similar autoloader, which appears to be based on Russian technology.

Both the commander and the gunner have roof mounted sights; these are stabilised and incorporate second generation light intensification imagers for use at night. As in the case of the Type 85-IIM, the Type 85-III can engage moving targets whilst on the move.

MOBILITY

A new powerpack offering substantially higher performance has been fitted, as has an automatic transmission. The high power to weight ratio should give excellent mobility. The manufacturers claim that the engine can be replaced in the field in less than 40 minutes. This is less than the hour required for the M1 but longer than the time required to change the Leopard 2's powerpack.

ASSESSMENT

An impressive tank incorporating some of the latest technology, the Type 85-III is likely to be a more dangerous foe than earlier Chinese designs.

SERVICE STATUS

It is uncertain if the Type 85-III has gone into production yet.

(not all data is available)

Prototype:	Early 1990s
In service:	Ready for production, not yet in service
Crew:	3
Armament:	Main, 125mm smoothbore cannon. Secondary, coaxial 1 x 7.62mm MG, anti-aircraft 1 x 12,7mm MG
Combat weight:	41,700kg
Power-to-weight ratio:	23.98hp/t
Ground pressure:	Not available
Length gun forward:	Not available
Hull length:	Not available
Hull width:	3.40m
Height:	2.20m
Ground clearance:	Not available
Power pack:	V-type diesel of 1,000hp
Max road speed:	65km/h
Max range:	550-600 km, (estimate)
Fording:	Not available
Gradient:	60% (estimate)
Side slope:	40% (estimate)
Vertical obstacle:	Not available

Type 85-III   *(Courtesy of J. McKaughan)*

MANUFACTURER: CHINESE STATE ORDNANCE FACTORIES

BACKGROUND
Announced in 1991, the Type 90-II is the most sophisticated example of Chinese tank design. It incorporates substantial advances in all areas of a tank's fighting qualities.

PROTECTION
The tank's hull and turret are both of welded steel construction. However over the frontal arc of the tank – that portion of the vehicle which is at greatest threat – composite armour has been added. This armour, which is found on both turret and hull, is of modular construction. It can be removed if damaged or when superior armour modules become available. Only in the case of the French Leclerc and the Israeli Merkava III, have manufacturers assimilated modular armour over a larger portion of the tank's shell, from the onset of the design process.

The Type 90-II incorporates other features to assist in its survivability. These include smoke grenade dischargers, an anti-radiation lining and an automatic fire detection/suppression system.

FIREPOWER
The Type 90-II carries the same 125mm smoothbore cannon and autoloader as the Type 85-III. An improved fire control system is installed. This consolidates stabilised day/night sights, a commander's control panel, laser rangefinder and meteorological sensors, into an integrated whole. The Type 90-II is capable of engaging moving targets during the day or at night with a good chance of a first shot kill.

MOBILITY
A powerful 1,200hp diesel ensures an excellent power to weight ratio. The tank appears to have a torsion bar suspension, but further details of the running gear are unknown.

ASSESSMENT
The Type 90-II has brought to fruition all the advances of the last decade made in Chinese tank design. It is a heavier, better protected design than the Type 85-III, but has potentially greater mobility because of a more powerful engine. The tank is not yet in production in China; some elements of the design may be incorporated in a future Pakistani MBT. If put into production the Type 90-II would be a dangerous opponent on the battlefield.

SERVICE STATUS
The tank is still being evaluated and is not in production.

(not all data is available)

Prototype:	1991
In service:	Not yet in service
Crew:	3
Armament:	Main, 125mm smoothbore cannon. Secondary, coaxial 1 x 7.62mm MG, anti-aircraft 1 x 12.7mm MG
Combat weight:	48,000kg
Power-to-weight ratio:	25hp/t
Ground pressure:	Not available
Length gun forward:	Not available
Hull length:	7.0m
Hull width:	3.4m
Height:	2m
Ground clearance:	Not available
Power pack:	A six or eight cylinder engine of 1,200hp coupled to an automatic' transmission
Max road speed:	60 km
Max range (internal fuel):	400 km
Fording:	Not available
Gradient:	60%
Side slope:	40%, (estimated)
Vertical obstacle:	0.85m

French post-war tank design initially mirrored that of Germany. Tanks reliant on their speed and agility rather than ballistic protection for their survival. The AMX-30, was lighter than most Western tanks but enjoyed comparable firepower and above average mobility. This approach remained valid in an era when conventional armour seemed unlikely to shield a tank against HEAT projectiles. Once sophisticated armour became available that offered a reasonable chance of protection against HEAT, then French design, as with other Western manufacturers, gave greater emphasis to protection, even at the expense of increased weight. Whilst it is true that French tank design originally fell behind that of other Western manufacturers, with the Leclerc France has introduced a tank at the cutting edge of armour technology. It was France that pioneered modular armour and an autoloader on Western MBTs, not her NATO rivals.

MANUFACTURER: GIAT INDUSTRIES

BACKGROUND

The AMX-30 owes its origins to a 1957 joint project with West Germany. The intention of the undertaking was to produce a standard tank to be used by the two countries. As is well known the joint endeavour failed and the two countries went their separate ways. The Germans went on to build the Leopard 1 and the French the AMX-30.

The AMX-30 was introduced into service in 1966 and produced until 1993. It will remain the premier MBT of the French army until the Leclerc is available in numbers.

PROTECTION

The tank has a rolled steel shell of welded construction. The armour is a little on the thin side, the hull in particular, is thinner than that of its closest competitor, the Leopard 1. The designers intended that the tank would depend on speed, agility and low silhouette for survival. Whilst it is true that the battlefield signature of the AMX-30's sleek hull and turret are small, the effect is spoiled by a high, and over complex commander's cupola.

Some efforts have been made to increase the tank's level of protection. The AMX-30 B2 variant of 1979 has thicker armour on the gun mantelet, and the option of fitting extra armour to the hull sides and attaching side skirts. Four battalions of AMX-30s in French service have been equipped to carry a reactive armour suite that offers greatly improved protection against HEAT rounds.

FIREPOWER

The AMX-30 carries a 105 mm rifled cannon, not the usual British L7 model, but the French built CN-105-F1. The gun is stabilised. The gun is fitted with a thermal shroud, but lacks the characteristic fume extractor of the British weapon. The gun relies on a compressed air supply to drive out fumes after it has fired. Advanced rounds for the gun, including depleted uranium penetrators, have been manufactured. The tank carries 47 rounds of ammunition, 18 in the turret. As well as the main armament, the AMX carries a 20mm coaxial weapon. This light cannon is very useful against soft targets and low flying, slow, aerial targets.

The baseline AMX-30s were furnished with a rather complex but effective system for sighting and gun laying. The AMX-30 B2 has an improved fire control system

French AMX-30 MBT heading towards the camera.   *(Courtesy of Will Fowler)*

Line up of French AMX-30 MBTs.

(Courtesy of John Norris)

French AMX-30 B2 with explosive reactive armour modules.

(Courtesy of John Norris)

that integrates a laser rangefinder and thermal camera, to increase speed and accuracy of gun laying.

MOBILITY

The basic tank has a multi-fuel engine that has been designed to be fairly easy to replace in the field. A torsion bar suspension is fitted, and the first and last of the five rubber tyred road wheels on each side have hydraulic shop absorbers. German critics state that the tanks ride is inferior to that of their Leopard 1, the tank that grew out of the same service requirement.

The AMX-30 B2 was provided with an improved gearbox and torsion bar suspension, to assist with a better cross-country ride.

ASSESSMENT

The AMX-30 is a low-slung fighting machine. By the standards of its contemporaries, it had fair protection, average firepower and good mobility. The AMX-30 was a reasonable design for its time and sold well, however it has aged badly and has fallen behind some of its contemporaries, particularly in terms of survivability.

SERVICE STATUS

The AMX-30 MBT is in service with Abu Dhabi, 95 tanks. Chile, 19. Cyprus, 52 AMX-30 B2. France, 947 AMX-30

of which 658 are of AMX-30 B2 standard, mostly rebuilds of older models. Qatar 24. Saudi Arabia 290 AMX-30S (the standard AMX-30 optimised for desert warfare), many of these tanks are in storage. Spain, 210. Venezuela, 70.

Prototype:	1960
In service:	1966
Crew:	4
Armament:	Main, 105mm rifled cannon. Secondary, coaxial 1 x 20mm cannon, anti-aircraft 1 x 7.62mm MG
Combat weight:	36,000kg (AMX-30). 37,000kg (AMX-30 B2)
Power-to-weight ratio:	20hp/t (AMX-30). 18.91hp (AMX-30 B2)
Ground pressure:	0.77kg/cm² (AMX-30). 0.90kg/cm² (AMX-30 B2)
Length gun forward:	9.48m
Hull length:	6.59m
Hull width:	3.1m
Height (to top of commander's cupola and searchlight):	2.86m
Ground clearance:	0.44m
Power pack:	Hispano-Suiza HS110 multi-fuel V-12 liquid cooled diesel of 720hp coupled to a mechanical trans- mission. The AMX-30 B2 is fitted with a modified model of the engine with improved turbo-chargers
Max road speed:	65km/h
Max range (internal fuel):	500km (AMX-30). 400km (AMX-30 B2)
Fording (unprepared):	1.2m
Gradient:	60%
Side slope:	30%
Vertical obstacle:	0.93m

MANUFACTURER: GIAT INDUSTRIES

BACKGROUND

There was an obvious need to replace the ageing AMX-30, and French industry was determined to produce a fighting vehicle at the forefront of tank design. The Leclerc demonstrates that they did so. The new tank incorporates integrated electronics on an unprecedented scale to increase its battlefield capabilities. Its protection, firepower and mobility all show dramatic advancement over its predecessor. First entering into production in 1991, the Leclerc is likely to be a presence on the battlefield for many years to come, as it has been deliberately constructed in a manner to assist upgrading.

PROTECTION

The Leclerc has detachable/replaceable modular armour. This allows the survivability of the tank to be increased as advances in armour technology become available. The armour modules used are advanced laminates which, it is claimed, offer the same level of protection as Chobham. Protection against mine explosion and top-attack is also better than most tanks.

The tank has a low silhouette and correspondingly small battlefield signature. If detected and fired upon, the tank has nine launchers built into each side of its turret. These can launch a variety of smoke grenades, decoys and anti-personnel warheads.

FIREPOWER

The tank carries a French 120mm smooth bore cannon that fires a number of advanced rounds. Anti-helicopter, and depleted uranium APFSDS rounds, are thought to be under development. The calibre length of the cannon is 52 compared to the more usual 44 adopted by most Western 120mm cannon designs; this gives a higher velocity for kinetic energy rounds. Firepower is enhanced by an integrated electronic battlefield management system. This links target acquisition, gun laying and automatic navigation equipment into a co-ordinated whole. Laser range finding, thermal imaging and stabilised sights, are integral to the system. The Leclerc's computer can engage up to five separate targets in less than a minute. The tank can fire accurately against both stationary and moving targets whilst the Leclerc itself is on the move. The Leclerc's crew have superior situational awareness thanks to the electronic suite. This gives a better chance of a first shot/first kill capability.

Leclerc frontal shot.   *(Courtesy of Will Fowler)*

Close up of Tropicalised Leclerc's turret. *(Courtesy of John Norris)*

Tropicalised Leclerc MBT. *(Courtesy of John Norris)*

As well as its comprehensive electronics, the Leclerc is the first NATO tank to have an automatic loader and a three-man crew. The autoloader is positioned in the tank's bustle and has 22 ready rounds; the autoloader can fire 10 rounds a minute. The gunner can also manually load 18 rounds stored in a drum to the right of the driver.

MOBILITY
The tanks diesel engine is unusual, incorporating features characteristic of a turbine – for example rapid acceleration. The resultant high power to weight ratio is utilised to the maximum by a hydropneumatic suspension.

ASSESSMENT
The Leclerc is one of the most advanced and formidable MBTs in service. It combines an imposing level of protection, impressive firepower, and a high power to weight ratio. The Leclerc also uses electronics to enhance its fighting qualities. It stands amongst a select group of tank designs, which compete for the title of the best MBT in current service.

SERVICE STATUS
The tank is entering into French service – an initial order is for 178 tanks. Abu Dhabi has ordered 436 Leclercs, optimised for desert conditions, and fitted with a German diesel.

Prototype:	1989
In service:	First delivery 1992, entering into full service, 1995
Crew:	3
Armament:	Main, 120mm smoothbore cannon. Secondary, coaxial 1 x 1 12.7mm MG, anti-aircraft 1 x 7.62mm MG
Combat weight:	54,500kg
Power-to-weight ratio:	27.52hp/t
Ground pressure:	0.9kg/cm^2
Length gun forward:	9.87m
Hull length:	6.88m
Hull width:	3.71m
Height (to turret roof):	2.53m
Ground clearance:	0.5m
Power pack:	SACEM UD V8X 1500 T9 Hyperbar 8-cylinder diesel of 1,500hp coupled to an automatic transmission
Max road speed:	71km
Max range (internal fuel):	550km
Fording (unprepared):	1.0m
Gradient:	60%
Side slope:	30%
Vertical obstacle:	1.3m

German post-war tank design has produced the exceptional Leopard series of MBTs. However there have been two distinct trends in the philosophy of German tank design. The Leopard 1 was built with a below average weight of armour, but with outstanding cross country mobility and good firepower. The Germans felt that as HEAT warheads were potentially lethal – unless a tank carried a crippling weight of armour – then battlefield survival should be sought through agility and speed. The lessons of successive Arab/Israeli wars, and the arrival of improved armour, led the Germans to adopt a more balanced tank design with Leopard 2.

Leopard 2 gives a much higher emphasis to armoured protection than its predecessor. This is not achieved to the detriment of mobility, as could be suggested in the case of British and Israeli tank design. The Leopard 2 of course carries the German built 120mm cannon which has been used, in one form or another, by most Western manufacturers.

MANUFACTURER: KRAUSS-MAFFEI & MaK

BACKGROUND

The Leopard tank grew out of a failed project run by France and West Germany in the 1950s to develop a joint MBT. The two countries went their separate ways, France to produce the AM-30 and Germany the Leopard 1 series of MBTs. The Leopard was built with mobility and firepower as its main priorities; protection came a definite third among the major design criteria.

PROTECTION

The Leopard 1 reflects a design philosophy that originally set a requirement for a tank of 30,000kg. Although both prototypes and production models exceed this, Leopard 1 was intended to survive through agility and mobility, rather than through weight of armour.

Successive Leopard variants were subject to a series of armour upgrades, which in turn were retrofitted to earlier models. From the original model Leopard 1 to the last variants produced, weight increased by 6%, nearly all as a result of additional armour. The baseline

model, the Leopard 1 was given additional appliqué armour weighing some 760kg. This appliqué armour – which consisted of rubber-backed steel plate – is attached to the cast steel turret and gun shield. The Leopard in this guise is known as the Leopard 1A1A. The Leopard, from the 1A3 variant onwards, is equipped with a welded steel turret incorporating spaced armour. As well as increased protection, this gives the tank a more angular appearance. The last of the new-build Leopards, the 1A4, is to be further upgraded to the 1A5 standard with a fire detection/suppression system added to the fighting compartment.

Like most modern tanks the Leopard is fitted with a NBC system and smoke grenade dischargers.

FIREPOWER

The Leopard 1 is fitted with the ubiquitous British 105mm L7 rifled cannon. Some 60 rounds of 105mm ammunition can be carried. This gun gives effective firepower, particularly when used with advanced ammunition. From the Leopard 1A1A of 1971, the tank has had a thermal sleeve for the cannon, and an efficient gun stabilisation

Leopard 1.   *(Courtesy of the manufacturer)*

system fitted. These increase accuracy and allow fire on the move. From 1986, the Leopard 1A5 has introduced an advanced, integrated fire control system that incorporates thermal imaging.

MOBILITY
Since its entry into service the Leopard 1, with its relatively low weight, has proved an exceptionally agile machine. A powerful diesel of 830hp and a torsion bar suspension system are standard. The power pack remained the same throughout the successive models of the tank, although from the Leopard 1A4 of 1974, an automatic transmission was installed as standard.

ASSESSMENT
The Leopard 1 is a competent design in a compact package and has deservedly sold well on the world market. It blends firepower and mobility as its prime characteristics; protection comes third. However clashes between armour since World War II, suggest a different order of priorities. It appears that as lethality of firepower has increased, then tank survivability has been best served through increased armoured protection, rather than through superior speed and mobility.

SERVICE STATUS
Australia has 90 tanks in service. Belgium, 334 tanks, some in store. Canada, 114 tanks. Denmark, 230 tanks. Germany, 731 tanks plus others in storage. Greece, 356 tanks. Italy (licence built), 910 tanks. Netherlands, 296 tanks in storage. Norway, 170 tanks. Turkey, 77 tanks.

Prototype:	1960
In service:	1965
Crew:	4
Armament:	Main, 105mm L7 cannon. Secondary, coaxial 1 x 7.62mm MG, anti-aircraft 1x 1 7.62mm MG
Combat weight:	Leopard 1 – 40,00kg. Leopard models 1A1, 1A1A1, 1A1A2 – 41,500kg. Leopard 1A2, 1A3, 1A4, 1A5 – 42,400kg.
Power-to-weight ratio:	Leopard 1 – 20.75hp/t. Later variants – 19.57hp/t
Ground pressure:	Leopard 1, 0.86kg/cm^2 Later variants, 0.89kg/cm^2
Length gun forward:	9.54m
Hull length:	7.09m
Hull width:	3.41m
Height (to commander's cupola):	2.613m. Later variants, 2.76m
Ground clearance:	0.44m
Power pack:	MTU MB 838 Ca M-500 V-10, liquid cooled diesel of 830hp coupled to an automatic transmission on late model tanks
Max road speed:	65km/h
Max range (internal fuel):	560km
Fording (unprepared):	1.2m
Gradient:	60%
Side slope:	30%
Vertical obstacle:	1.15m

MANUFACTURER: KRAUSS MAFFEI & MaK

BACKGROUND

The Leopard 2 grew from an abortive attempt by the USA and West Germany to design a common MBT. The US went on to build the M1 and Germany the Leopard 2. The Leopard 2 was built to very different design criteria than Leopard 1; a much greater emphasis was given to protection and survivability. The Leopard 2 is one of the most formidable of modern MBTs. It has been built in six models with minor variations in capability, and one, the Leopard 2 (Improved), which has significant changes.

PROTECTION

The Leopard 2 is all of 38% heavier than the Leopard 1 and is a much more heavily protected vehicle. At least 10% of that weight gain was for further armour, as the lessons of the 1973 Arab/Israeli war were incorporated by the Leopard 2 design team. The tank uses spaced composite armour on both its hull and turret. In 1990 a major rebuild of the standard tank known as the Leopard 2 (Improved) was initiated. The Leopard 2 (Improved) has additional protection in the form of replaceable and upgradable armoured modules attached to its frontal arc. The turret mantle in particular – with its new wedge shaped profile is better shielded.

The tank has a collective NBC system and in the latest models, a spall liner for its crew compartment. From the Leopard 2A4 onwards, a fire detection/suppression system was incorporated as standard.

FIREPOWER

The Leopard 2 introduced the Rheinmetall 120mm smoothbore cannon. This weapon has supplanted the British 105mm rifled weapon as the most commonly used by modern Western tanks. The Leopard 2 carries some 42 rounds of ammunition for its main cannon.

Successive variants of the Leopard 2 have introduced improvements in their fire control system. The Leopard 2A1 introduced a thermal imaging capability, which replaces earlier image intensifiers. The fire control of Leopard 2 (Improved) incorporates some advances. These include an enhanced capability to engage helicopters and an independent thermal channel for the commander's monitor.

Latest model Leopard 2 (Improved), note re-profiled turret front.   *(Courtesy of the manufacturer)*

MOBILITY

The Leopard 2, despite its bulk, has an excellent power-to-weight ratio. A new multi-fuel, turbocharged diesel, gives 1,500hp. The engine gives an 80% increase in power when compared to that of the Leopard 1 and is linked to an automatic transmission. Despite the considerable rise in weight over the Leopard 1, the Leopard 2 still has a comparative 30% improvement in its power to weight ratio. The torsion bar suspension has friction dampers that allow an increase in speed over rough terrain.

ASSESSMENT

Having shifted their design goals to give greater attention to protection, the Germans have produced a superb MBT. It is possibly the best MBT in service at the time of publication.

Not only is survivability excellent, but both firepower and mobility are formidable.

SERVICE STATUS

Germany is the major user with 1,964 in service of which 225 are in the process of being upgraded to the Leopard 2 (Improved) model. Other users are the Netherlands, 444 tanks. Spain, 108 tanks, delivery in progress. Sweden, 160 tanks, others to be assembled locally. Switzerland, 380 tanks.

Prototype:	1973
In service:	1979
Crew:	4
Armament:	Main, 120mm smoothbore cannon. Secondary, coaxial 1 x 7.62mm MG, anti-aircraft 1 x 7.62mm MG
Combat weight:	55,150kg. Leopard 2 (Improved) 59,000kg
Power-to-weight ratio:	27hp/t. Leopard 2 (Improved): 25.5hp/t
Ground pressure:	0.83kg/cm^2
Length gun forward:	9.67m
Hull length:	7.66m
Hull width:	3.7m
Height (to commander's cupola):	2.78m
Ground clearance:	0.49m
Power pack:	MTU MB 837 Ka-501 multi-fuel, turbocharged diesel of 1,500hp coupled to an automatic transmission
Max road speed:	72km/h
Max range (internal fuel):	550km
Fording (unprepared):	1.0m
Gradient:	60%
Side slope:	30%
Vertical obstacle:	1.1m

MANUFACTURER: KRAUSS-MAFFEI

BACKGROUND

Although referred to as an MBT by its manufacturer, the Puma is closer to a medium tank in the class of the TH 301. The tank's hull is that of the Puma Armoured Combat Vehicle family, its turret that of surplus Leopard 1 tanks. The vehicle has a front mounted engine with all the resultant advantages of that configuration. In the case of the Puma this includes the capacity to carry four infantrymen in a space by its rear access doors.

Several variants of the Puma have been under development since 1993, ranging in purpose from IFVs to tank killers. All share a baseline configuration but with different weights, ranging from 25 to 40 tonnes. The heavier vehicles have more powerful engines and different running gear to cope with the increased weight. The Puma tank variant, shown for the first time in 1994, has a good blend of protection, firepower and mobility.

PROTECTION

An all-welded steel hull and turret are able to defeat armour piercing heavy machine gun rounds. The turret has a layer of spaced armour, and both hull and turret could be given further protection through appliqué passive or reactive armour. The layout of the tank with a front mounted engine helps increase crew survivability. Firstly the engine adds its mass to help protect the crew compartment. Secondly, if a crew does have to abandon its tank, then they are able bale out in relative safety from the Puma's rear door.

Fire detection/suppression equipment is fitted as standard, as is an NBC system.

FIREPOWER

The Puma tank prototypes are fitted with turrets from surplus Leopard 1A5 tanks. These mount a fully stabilised 105mm rifled cannon, plus fire control unusually advanced for a tank of the Puma's weight class. The system is based on that of the Leopard 2; it integrates stabilised day/night sights with a laser rangefinder and also incorporates thermal imaging. The tank commander has his own sophisticated optics, giving him a surveillance capability distinct from that of the gunner. Of the 61 rounds of ammunition, none are carried above the level of the turret ring.

Puma MBT moving at speed.   *(Courtesy of the manufacturer)*

MOBILITY

The tank carrying less weight than Leopard 1, has a better power to weight ratio. The torsion bar suspension system – borrowing technology from the Leopard 2 – uses hydrodynamic bump stops which give the Puma a superior ride when compared to the Leopard 1.

ASSESSMENT

The Puma is an impressive design. In particular it has firepower and gunnery control, at a level of sophistication not usually associated with a vehicle of the Puma's weight. By using the maximum number of components already in wide spread service, the manufacturer has reduced costs and increased reliability. The use of the Leopard 1 turret increases the Puma's potential pool of buyers, the Leopard 1 being one of the best selling post-war tanks.

SERVICE STATUS

Not yet in service, awaiting orders.

Prototype:	1994
In service:	Not yet in service
Crew:	4 (The vehicle can also carry 4 infantrymen in its rear compartment)
Armament:	Main, 105mm rifled cannon. Secondary, coaxial 1 x 7.62mm MG
Combat weight:	36,000kg
Power-to-weight ratio:	20.83hp/t
Ground pressure:	0.74kg/cm^2
Length gun forward:	Not available
Hull length:	6.50m
Hull width:	3.25m
Height (to turret roof):	2.55m
Ground clearance:	0.44m
Power pack:	MAN D 2840 LE V10 diesel of 750hp coupled to an automatic transmission
Max road speed:	70km/h
Max range (internal fuel):	650km
Fording (unprepared):	1.2m
Gradient:	60%
Side slope:	30%
Vertical obstacle:	0.91m

MANUFACTURER: THYSSEN HENSCHEL

BACKGROUND
The TH 301 is closely based on the TAM light tank developed for Argentina. Both the TAM and TH 301 use the chassis and components of the Marder IFV. The chassis of the TH 301 has been designed to be more robust than that of the standard Marder, both to cope with its increased weight and the recoil of its heavier weapon.

The TAM prototype was completed in 1976. The prototype of the TH 301 family, closely based upon its TAM predecessor, was completed in 1978. The TH 301 has been offered for sale since the early 1980s.

PROTECTION
The all-welded hull and turret have well thought out shapes, optimised to provide maximum ballistic protection. The glacis offers protection against light cannon of up to 40mm calibre. The vehicle's low height helps it to avoid detection and destruction on the battlefield, as do its smoke grenade launchers. The front mounted engine allows a rear door to be fitted, enabling the crew to bail out of a damaged vehicle whilst protected by its hull. The engine itself helps to protect the crew compartment from being pierced by projectiles penetrating the vehicle's frontal arc.

FIREPOWER
The TH 301 carries a German built 105mm rifled cannon; replacement options include a 35mm or 57mm weapon. The main difference between the TAM and the TH 301 is the latter's more comprehensive and sophisticated fire control, based on that of the late model Leopard 1. Both commander and gunner have stabilised periscopes, a digital computer is fitted as is a laser rangefinder, and a LLTV camera is fitted for night targeting.

Up to 50 rounds are carried for the main weapon. The rear door allows rapid resupply of ammunition.

MOBILITY
A more powerful power pack than that of the TAM is installed on the TH 301. This gives a superior power to weight ratio. Like the TAM the TH 301 is an agile combat vehicle with a reasonably low ground pressure and torsion bar suspension.

TH 301 tank. *(Courtesy of the manufacturer)*

ASSESSMENT

The TH 301 is a very useful combat vehicle. Wherever possible the components of the successful Marder IFV series have been used, to maximise reliability and ease maintainability.

SERVICE STATUS

The TH 301 family has not gained any orders, other than for the TAM sale to Argentina.

Prototype:	1978
In service:	Not yet in service
Crew:	4
Armament:	Main, 105mm rifled cannon. Secondary, coaxial 1 x 7.62mm MG, anti-aircraft 1 x 7.62mm MG
Combat weight:	31,000kg
Power-to-weight ratio:	24.2hp/t
Ground pressure:	0.74kg/cm^2
Length gun forward:	8.45m
Hull length:	6.72m
Hull width:	3.30m
Height (to turret top):	2.43m
Ground clearance:	0.45m
Power pack:	MTU MB 833 Ka-500 supercharged diesel of 720hp coupled to a hydraulic shift transmission
Max road speed:	72km/h
Max range (internal fuel):	500km
Fording (unprepared):	1.4m
Gradient:	60%
Side slope:	30%
Vertical obstacle:	1.0m

MANUFACTURER: HEAVY VEHICLES FACTORY, AVADI

BACKGROUND
In 1961, after a process of competitive tender, India began the licensed production of the Vickers Defence Systems Mk 1 MBT (see relevant entry). The Indian variant, known as the Vijayanta, was built in numbers – 2,200 being assembled between 1965 and 1983. The original Vijayanta was very closely based on the Vickers Mk 1, however over the years, adaptations to local conditions and needs, saw changes develop between the baseline Mk 1 and the late model Vijayanta. As the production of India's indigenous tank the Arjun has been delayed on a number of occasions, India is to upgrade between 400 and 1,100 of its Vijayanta fleet. The improved vehicle is known as the Bison.

PROTECTION
The protection offered by the Vijayanta is that of the Vickers Mk 1. It has a well-sloped glacis but armour thinner than that of larger, heavier, more expensive MBTs. The Bison upgrade is to be fitted with appliqué, composite, passive armour.

FIREPOWER
The standard weapon is the British L7 105mm rifled cannon. The original fire control and targeting system was that of the Vickers Mk 1. Just as that tank's fire control system was successively modernised, so the Vijayanta followed the same pattern. The ranging machine gun has been replaced by laser range finders and ballistic computers. The Bison upgrade will incorporate new fire control systems including passive night sights and, possibly, thermal imaging.

MOBILITY
The Vijayanta was initially fitted with the same power pack as the early Vickers Mk 1. Some 400 Vijayanta are to be fitted with a German MTU Series 837 V-8 diesel of 750hp. The Bison is to be fitted with an indigenous engine based on that of the T-72. (India has produced the T-72 under licence since 1988. The T-72 replaces the Vijayanta as India's most powerful tank, until the Arjun enters into service).

Vijayanta, in Indian camouflage.　　　　　　　　　　　　　　　*(Courtesy of the Tank Museum)*

ASSESSMENT

The Vijayanta has proved a capable MBT in Indian hands. It has a high degree of built-in 'stretch' and is easy to upgrade; the main constraint has been available resources. Only in Indian service, some 2,200 have been produced. A declining number of gun tanks remain on the inventory, as hulls are used as the basis for a series of specialised variants. Hulls have been used to construct a number of self-propelled guns, armoured recovery vehicles and assault bridges.

SERVICE STATUS

India still has at least 800 Vijayanta tanks in service.

(The basic Vijayanta is much the same as the Vickers Mk 1 but with the following differences in specifications)

Prototype:	1963
In service:	1965
Combat weight:	40,400kg
Power-to-weight ratio:	With Leyland engine – 16.089hp/t. With MTU diesel – 18.564hp/t
Length gun forward:	9.788m
Height (to commander's cupola):	2.711m
Power pack:	The original engine is the Leyland L60 Mk 4 of 650hp coupled to a semi-automatic transmission. The MTU 837 V-8 diesel of 750hp may be fitted to some tanks
Max road speed:	48.3km/h
Max range (internal fuel):	350-400km/h
Fording (unprepared):	1.3m
Vertical obstacle:	0.914m

MANUFACTURER: HEAVY VEHICLES FACTORY, AVADI

BACKGROUND
Arjun is India's first indigenous MBT, and has undergone a prolonged development process with many setbacks. The design project was launched in 1974, the first prototype unveiled in 1985, and entry into service delayed until the late 1990s. The tank incorporates many advanced technologies. It has proven difficult for its manufacturers, to develop and integrate various complex components into a functioning vehicle. A series of 20 prototypes and further pre-production vehicles are being trialled by the manufacturers and the Indian Army.

PROTECTION
The tank has the slab-sided, angular turret typical of advanced composite armours. The Indians have developed their own laminated special armour known as Kanchan. The first six prototypes of the Arjun were built out of mild steel, the special armour requiring time to come to fruition.

The tank has an NBC system and smoke grenade launchers to enhance prospects of battlefield survival.

FIREPOWER
The Arjun is fitted with a 120mm cannon developed locally. India like Britain has chosen a rifled weapon rather than a smooth bore gun. The cannon fires a range of Indian designed ammunition, the gun itself is stabilised and fitted with a thermal sleeve. Fire control is sophisticated, incorporating a laser rangefinder, thermal imaging, stabilised panoramic sights for the tank commander, meteorological sensors, and a ballistic computer. The combination gives the tank a high probability of successfully engaging moving or stationary targets whilst the Arjun itself is on the move.

MOBILITY
Providing an adequate power pack for the Arjun has proved to be difficult. The tank weighs in at approximately 58,000kg. An attempt to develop a gas turbine failed and, despite help from German companies, constructing a locally designed diesel engine of 1,500hp has been problematical. A quantity of German MTU water cooled diesels of 1,400hp has been purchased to power the prototypes. These are also likely to power initial production standard Arjuns.

The tank is intended to use an advanced hydro-pneumatic suspension and be capable of speeds over 70km/h.

ASSESSMENT
The Arjun, if it ever enters into service, will be a very impressive and capable tank. It is unclear at present if the tank will be built in large numbers. The manufacturers are attempting to integrate a large number of advanced components; this has led to problems with reliability and maintainability. Financial constraints have not eased the situation. It is possible that India may decide to drop the Arjun, the project proving too ambitious, and licence build a foreign design.

SERVICE STATUS
Not yet in service; in development.

SPECIFICATIONS
Other than the information given in the text, no other reliable data is available.

Stationary Arjun.   *(Courtesy of Lt Col P Flach)*

MANUFACTURER: TEXTRON MARINE AND LAND SYSTEMS/CHINA NATIONAL MACHINERY AND EQUIPMENT IMPORT AND EXPORT CORPORATION

BACKGROUND

This interesting venture blends advanced technology from an American company with the basic Chinese Type 59 tank. The result is a potentially very capable vehicle. The tank is intended for the export market, where it would be a tempting proposition for developing states. The project was launched in 1988 and the prototype was up and running in 1989. Political developments have placed restrictions on the joint project developing further. Textron hope to use the technology and knowledge gained from the programme, not just for new build vehicles, but also for the potentially lucrative upgrade market.

PROTECTION

Appliqué armour, probably a passive compound material, has been applied to the hull and turret of the basic Type 59. Rubber side skirts cover the upper portion of the running gear. To what extent overall protection is increased is classified. As the Jaguar weighs 6,000kg more than the Type 59, it is likely to be considerable.

The tank is equipped with a fire detection/ suppression system and smoke grenade launchers as standard; an optional NBC system can be fitted.

FIREPOWER

The main gun is a fully stabilised 105mm rifled cannon, complete with a thermal sleeve. The fire control integrates image intensification night sights, with laser rangefinding, and is sufficiently sophisticated to accurately engage moving targets, whilst the tank itself is on the move. The digital fire control system is built by British Marconi Radar and Control Systems, and is the same as fitted to the Stingray light tank delivered to Thailand.

MOBILITY

The Jaguar has a 750hp engine that gives it considerably greater agility than the original Type 59, despite its increase in weight. The suspension is of an improved torsion bar type. If required, Textron can replace the standard, Chinese track with a more durable substitute. An improved ride over rough terrain can be obtained by fitting an optional hydropneumatic suspension.

ASSESSMENT

The Jaguar project has been threatened by political developments, both in terms of US/China relations and by the Conventional Forces in Europe treaty (CFE). Tanks surplus to CFE limitations have been offered at knock-down prices to potential customers. However the fact that the technology of the Jaguar project can be retrofitted to obsolete Type 59 and T-54/55 tanks, should still attract interest.

SERVICE STATUS

Not yet in service, awaiting orders.

Prototype:	1989
In service:	Not yet in service
Crew:	4
Armament:	Main, 105mm rifled cannon. Secondary, coaxial 1 x 7.62mm MG, anti-aircraft 1 x 12.7mm MG
Combat weight:	42,000kg
Power-to-weight ratio:	17.9hp/t
Ground pressure:	0.98kg/cm²
Length gun forward:	9.6m
Hull length:	6.8m
Hull width:	3.27m
Height (to commander's cupola):	2.63m
Ground clearance:	Not available
Power pack:	Detroit Diesel 8V-92TA 8 cylinder diesel of 750hp coupled to an automatic transmission
Max road speed:	55km/h
Max range:	not available
Fording (unprepared):	1.1m
Gradient:	60%
Side slope:	30%
Vertical obstacle:	Not available

MANUFACTURER: IRAQI STATE ORDNANCE FACTORIES

BACKGROUND

The Iraqis have renovated many of their Soviet and Chinese supplied MBTs. In fact, most of what are usually referred to as Iraqi modified T-55s, are actually ex-Chinese Type 59 and Type 69 tanks. Most of the modifications are concerned with improving the tank's level of protection and battlefield survivability.

PROTECTION

During the Gulf War, Allied forces encountered a small number of T-55 type tanks with heavy passive appliqué armour. The stand-off armour is made up of laminated material, incorporating steel and rubber sandwiched together in metal boxes. The armour is intended to give a high degree of protection over the frontal arc of both hull and turret. A large counterweight is fitted to the turret rear to compensate for the additional weight on the tank's front. The counterweight itself acts as additional stand-off protection for the turret rear. The configuration is crude and unwieldy, but likely to be effective against HEAT projectiles.

FIREPOWER

Although the modified variants mentioned above maintained their original weapon, some Iraqi T-55 class tanks have been up-gunned. Type 69 tanks have been observed with 125mm guns of the type carried by the T-72. These tanks have also had the autoloader from the T-72 installed; this gives their turrets a raised and altered profile.

MOBILITY

Those Iraqi tanks fitted with heavy appliqué armour retain the same engine, thus they have reduced agility. A small number of Iraqi tanks may have been upgraded with kits supplied by Romania. The kits include a more powerful 620hp power pack.

ASSESSMENT

Although unrefined and somewhat rustic in appearance, Iraqi modified T-55 class tanks, do have improved protection. However, the Gulf War demonstrated that survivability of the modified T-55 remains marginal, when faced with a sophisticated opponent.

SERVICE STATUS

Nubers in service unknown.

SPECIFICATIONS

No accurate information available.

Captured Iraqi T-55 upgraded with applique armour consisting of a metal alloy and rubber sandwich.
Note armour modules on the sides of hull and turret plus the clumsy counterweight on the turret rear. *(Courtesy of the Tank Museum)*

Israeli tank design has, even more than in the case of Britain, concentrated on protection at the expense of reduced mobility. Their recent history of armoured warfare has convinced the Israelis that their priority should be to preserve the lives of their tank crew. Much thought has been given to the configuration of the Merkava MBT. The front mounted engine allows all the components of this heavily armoured tank to contribute to the protection of the crew compartment. Despite it being under powered, the Israelis believe that the waddling but formidably protected Merkava maintains real battlefield manoeuvrability.

Apart from developing the Merkava range of MBTs, the Israelis have proved themselves masters of upgrading obsolete tanks, squeezing the maximum use from elderly designs.

MANUFACTURER: ISRAELI ORDNANCE FACTORIES

BACKGROUND

The Israeli developed M51 Isherman is a Second World War Sherman tank, upgraded so that it could successfully combat Soviet T-54/55 series MBTs. Firepower and mobility were considerably improved over the baseline Sherman. The M51 is now long obsolete, but in the Arab/Israeli wars of 1967 and 1973 it engaged and destroyed much more modern armour.

PROTECTION

The armour protection of the M51 is that of the basic Sherman, with all the problems associated with that tanks relatively thin armour. The replacement of its petrol engine with a diesel one means that the tank is less prone to brew up if hit. The M51 is also fitted with smoke grenade dischargers in an attempt to improve battlefield survivability.

FIREPOWER

The M51 carries an adaptation of a French 105mm 56 calibre cannon. The new cannon, the D1504, had its calibre reduced to 44, and in consequence a reduction of its muzzle velocity from 1000m/s to 800m/s. After these changes the shorter more manageable cannon could be mounted on the M51 in a heavily modified turret. The turret required an elongated counter-weight at its rear, to compensate for the new gun's increase in weight.

Ammunition for the gun was built locally, the main tank killer being HEAT rounds. Firing HEAT projectiles, the new weapon could penetrate the shell of a T-54/55 from all angles, and could even penetrate the thick armour of the Soviet built IS-III.

MOBILITY

The hull of the Sherman was stripped and a completely new power pack and running gear was fitted. The original petrol engine was replaced by a diesel, the transmission modified and an E8 HVSS suspension fitted along with wider tracks. In the aftermath of all these changes the M51 had an increased combat weight, but retained comparable speed with, and a better ride than, the baseline Sherman.

ASSESSMENT

The M51 is a good example of how an obsolete tank can be given a new lease of life, through careful renovation and upgrading. Although no longer viable on a high intensity battlefield, the M51 gave sterling service in times of war.

SERVICE STATUS

The tank is no longer in service with Israeli units. A few M51 MBTs may be in storage, but the hulls of the majority were used as the basis of engineer vehicles and self-propelled artillery. Some 150 M51 tanks were supplied to Chile where they are now in storage.

M51 photographed from the side, showing its French made/ Israeli modified 105 mm cannon to advantage. Note counter- weight to the turret rear. *(Copyright of Marsh Gelbart)*

(available data as follows)

Prototype:	1960
In service:	1965/66
Crew:	4
Armament:	Main, 105mm rifled cannon, coaxial 1 x 7.62mm MG, anti-aircraft 1 x 12.7mm MG
Combat weight:	39,000kg
Power-to-weight ratio:	11.79hp/t
Power pack:	Cummins diesel of 460hp coupled to a manual transmission
Max road speed:	45km/h
Max range (internal fuel):	270km

MANUFACTURER: ISRAELI ORDNANCE CORPS

BACKGROUND
Purchased by Israel in 1960, the early British built Mark 3 and 5 Centurions were dated and unreliable. However after a process of continual upgrading, Centurion based MBTs proved the most effective of Israel's tanks in the wars of 1967 and 1973. The Sho't, an extensive modification of the Centurion tank, appeared in Israeli service in 1970.

PROTECTION
In response to the growing threat of infantry launched HEAT warheads – as demonstrated in the 1973 Middle East war – the Israelis developed an explosive reactive armour known as Blazer. Blazer offers greatly improved protection against HEAT projectiles. Detachable modules of Blazer attached to the front hull and turret of the Sho't, proved effective in the Lebanon war of 1982.

The fitting of a low profile cupola and of new smoke grenade dischargers, helped to reduce the tank's battlefield signature and increase its survivability.

FIREPOWER
The dated 20 pdr cannon was replaced by a licence built 105mm British weapon from 1963. This new gun proved lethal in successive wars. The tank can carry up to 72 cannon shells. A refined fire control system incorporating laser rangefinding, image intensification night sights, and a digital computer was fitted to the Sho't from 1984.

MOBILITY
From 1967 the original Meteor petrol engine and its manual gearbox, were replaced by a more powerful, reliable, diesel engine and an automatic transmission. The new power pack (which entailed raising the engine decks), decreased driver fatigue and increased the tank's range.

ASSESSMENT
The Centurion's sound basic design and growth potential allowed significant improvement. The Sho't, although now obsolescent, proved capable of defeating tanks of a later generation. The tank's hull has provided the basis for a number of variants. The most interesting of which is a hybrid combat engineer vehicle/heavy APC, known as the Puma.

SERVICE STATUS
Until recently, up to 1,100 Sho'ts were in frontline service. Now most are in reserve, whilst an increasing number of Sho'ts are being converted to Puma combat engineer vehicles.

Sho't post 1982 version, front view. Note attachment points for Blazer reactive armour   *(Copyright of Marsh Gelbart)*

Puma APC conversion from Sho't. Note mine rollers.
(Copyright of Marsh Gelbart)

Sho't MBT fitted with Blazer reactive armour modules built by Rafael.   *(Courtesy of manufacturer)*

Puma combat engineer vehicle built on the hull of an Israli upgraded Centurion. Front right view. Note attachment of RKM mine rollers plus good view of special armour side-skirts.
(Copyright of Marsh Gelbart)

Prototype:	Modifications from baseline Centurion from 1960, Sho't prototype 1968/9
In service:	1970
Crew:	4
Armament:	Main, 105mm cannon. Secondary, coaxial 1 x 7.62mm MG, anti-aircraft 2 x 7.62mm MG. Additional, 1 x 12.7mm MG
Combat weight:	51,800kg (52,800 with Blazer)
Power-to-weight ratio:	14.48hp/t
Ground pressure:	not available
Length gun forward:	9.83m
Hull length:	7.8m
Hull width:	3.39m
Height (to commander's cupola):	2.96m
Ground clearance:	0.457m
Power pack:	TCM AVDS- 1790-2A V-12 diesel of 750hp coupled to an automatic transmission
Max road speed:	43km/h
Max range (internal fuel):	400km
Fording (unprepared):	1.45m
Gradient:	60%
Side slope:	40%
Vertical obstacle:	0.9m

Sho't moving directly towards the camera. Note this vehicle does not have reactive armour.
(Copyright of John Norris)

MANUFACTURER: ISRAELI ORDNANCE CORPS

BACKGROUND

The Israelis captured several hundred T54/55 tanks from Syria and Egypt in 1967 and 1973.

The small battlefield signature of the T-54/55, with its low mushroom shaped turret, and compact overall size, was an advantage. However the ensuing repercussions included cramped conditions and poor ergonomics. Numerous changes were made in order to enhance battlefield effectiveness. However the cramped fighting compartment endured by the crew was a constant problem.

PROTECTION

The ballistic protection of the baseline T-54/55 was reasonably good, the armour being thick and well sloped. However if the fighting compartment was pierced, there was the probability of a catastrophic explosion as on board ammunition was inadequately shielded. The Israelis fitted Blazer reactive armour to Tirans in the 1980s, along with fire detection and suppression systems, in an attempt to alleviate this problem.

External storage panniers were added to the turret sides and rear. These not only gave much needed space for kit, but gave a more angular appearance. This allowed the Tiran to be distinguished from the unmodified Soviet tanks used by Israel's enemies.

FIREPOWER

At first opportunity the Israelis replaced the inadequate 100mm gun with the excellent M68 105mm cannon. The Russian machine guns were also supplanted by Western models. A more sophisticated fire control system, incorporating laser rangefinding, second generation image intensifiers and a digital computer has been fitted in recent years. However no fix could be made for the vehicle's principal defect. Like many Soviet built tanks, the cannon has a limited range of depression. This inhibits the ability to fire from a hull-down position.

MOBILITY

The ultimate conversion of the T54/55 – sometimes referred to as the Tiran Model S – was announced in 1984. This model concentrated on improving mobility. It saw the fitting of a more powerful American engine, a semi-automatic transmission and replacement of the drivers steering rods with a steering wheel.

ASSESSMENT

The TI-67 Tiran was a brave attempt to squeeze the maximum fighting effectiveness from a tank restricted by its small size.

SERVICE STATUS

Only having seen service in Israeli colours, the Tiran is now obsolete as a battle tank. Some 300 Tirans are available, most in storage. Turretless Tirans are being modified into heavily protected Infantry Fighting Vehicles. These are known as the Achzarit.

The dimensions and performance of the TI-67 Tiran remain largely those of the T-55. Other than the attempt to improve crew comfort and install a superior fire-control system the main changes are as follows.

Armament:	Main, 105 M68 cannon. Secondary, coaxial 1x 7.62mm MG, Anti-aircraft, 1 x 7.62mm MG and 1 x 0.50 Browning MG
Power pack:	American General Motors 8V-71T diesel of 609hp
Power-to-weight ratio:	16.9hp/t

TI-67 Tiran, note 105 mm cannon.   *(Copyright of Marsh Gelbart)*

MANUFACTURER: ISRAELI ORDNANCE CORPS

BACKGROUND

The Israelis have a long history of re-engineering elderly tanks and improving their performance. Their definitive upgrade has involved the evolution of US M48 and M60 tanks – known in Israeli service as the Magach – into the Magach 7.

The Israelis were provided with an initial batch of M48s in 1965. These were second-hand machines that had already seen hard usage in the West German army and which were ripe for renovation. Newer M60s were purchased directly from the US in the 1970s.

PROTECTION

The initial batch of M48s was vulnerable. The petrol engine was prone to burst into flames when hit, and the Israelis substituted a diesel engine. A small number of these improved MBTs fought during the Six Day War of 1967.

One significant change the Israelis made to both the M48 and M60 was to remove the original, over-complex commander's cupola. It was replaced with a neat, low-profile design built by Urdan. The substitute reduced the tanks visible signature and thus increased its survivability.

By the late 1970s the Israelis were able to introduce a startling improvement to the Magach's survivability. Rectangular bricks of reactive armour known as Blazer were added to the turrets and hull of the Magach. Used in the 1982 Lebanon war, Blazer made the Magach highly resistant to infantry anti-tank weapons. Blazer involved a weight penalty of 800 to 1,000 pounds but gave protection equivalent to 10 tons of steel against HEAT warheads.

The survivability of the Magach's crew was further augmented. In the 1973 war the Israelis had noted that a high proportion of Magach crewmen suffered burns. These were caused by the flammable hydraulic fluid used in the Magach's turret mechanism. A fluid with a higher flash point was introduced to prevent this. Also a fire/explosion suppression system was fitted to the Magach's crew compartment which can prevent most incendiary flash fires.

One major problem with Blazer was that, unlike Chobham, it had little effect on kinetic energy weapons such as APDS. By the mid 1980s the Israelis had developed passive armour with a performance comparable to Chobham. The Magach 7 was fitted with this new armour and brought into service in 1989. The new armour fitted to the turret, to the front of the hull and to bazooka skirts shielding the tracks, gave a considerable increase to the tank's protection. The passive armour kits changed the profile of the Magach, giving it its slab sided, angular appearance.

Magach 7 slowing down as it approaches the camera.
(Copyright of Marsh Gelbart)

Magach post 1982, with reactive armour removed, note view of attachment points for the reactive armour.
(Copyright of Marsh Gelbart)

Magach post 1982 side view.   *(Copyright of Marsh Gelbart)*

FIREPOWER

The original M48 toting a 90mm gun was under armed, so Israel rapidly began to replace the American weapon with the British 105mm cannon produced under licence. The M60 came with this weapon fitted as standard. The Magach 7 was given more deadly firepower through the introduction of advanced ammunition. This included new APFSDS rounds to destroy enemy tanks, and a flechette shell for use against soft targets. An externally mounted 60mm mortar was fitted to the turret roof for use against enemy infantry. Greatly improved fire control, using a laser range finder and sophisticated thermal night sights, means that the Magach 7 can hold its own in combat against brand new tanks.

MOBILITY

The petrol engine of the original M48 had been replaced by a 750hp diesel that gave greater range. The M60 tanks bought by the Israelis directly from the US in the 1970s came equipped with a diesel engine. However the new passive armour of the Magach 7 added some five tons in weight. This necessitated further improvement in motive power. Mobility was maintained and indeed increased by fitting a more powerful diesel engine generating 908hp. The new engine was coupled to an advanced transmission to get the most from the new power pack. Manoeuvrability was further enhanced by the adoption of lighter, yet more rugged, tracks.

Israeli MBTs were also issued with engineering equipment to help enhance versatility and manoeuv-rability. Magach tanks are often fitted with dozer blades mounted onto their front plates. As well as the dozer blades the Magach is frequently equipped with attachment points for mine ploughs.

ASSESSMENT

The metamorphosis of the M48 to the Magach 7 took nearly thirty years to come to fruition. The continuous upgrade programme enabled an elderly tank to vastly increase its fighting ability. The Israelis have already trialled a Magach with a 120mm cannon, suggesting that there are further improvements afoot. The Magach 7 project shows that obsolete MBTs can, with skill and imagination, be developed into effective fighting machines.

SERVICE STATUS

There are some 400 up-rated M48s and 1,600 up-rated M60s in Israeli service. Of this combined figure it is expected that at least 400 will be improved to Magach 7 status.

Other than the improved fire control system and advanced armour, Magach 7 statistics are the same as the baseline M60, but with the following changes:

Combat weight:	54,000kg (M60 – 49,714kg)
Power-to-weight ratio:	16.8hp/t (M60 – 15.08hp/t)
Power pack:	TCM AVDS-1790-6A V-12 diesel of 908hp (M60 – Continental AVDS-1790-2A diesel of 750hp)

Magach 7, crewman waving.

(Copyright of Marsh Gelbart)

MANUFACTURER: ISRAELI ORDNANCE CORPS

BACKGROUND

The Merkava (MBT) developed by the Israelis throughout the 1970s and put in service in 1979, remains one of the most formidable of MBT's in current use. The influence of General Tal, an experienced combat officer, is directly responsible for many of the vehicles' innovations. The Merkava has a number of unique design features which boost its effectiveness and make it a very unusual beast.

Following the wars of June 1967 and October 1973, the Israelis decided that protection and survivability should be maximised at the expense of mobility. Israel had rediscovered an old lesson – that there was a difference in actual combat conditions between professed mobility, and real tactical manoeuvrability. A heavier machine may lumber around the combat zone slowly, when compared to its lighter more sprightly counterparts, however it can better survive on a fire saturated battlefield. Requests to buy Britain's Chieftain having been denied, the Israelis launched into the production of their own MBT – the Merkava.

The Israelis gave high priority to battle sustainability. The Merkava had to be easy to repair and maintain. It also had to carry an unusually large amount of ammunition so that it could continue to fight for a long period. Clever ergonomics – the science of adapting machinery to the comfort of its operators – helps reduce crew fatigue on the Merkava.

PROTECTION

Survivability of tanks and crew were given absolute priority; both were in short supply. Despite initially lacking certain modern technologies, such as Chobham armour, the Israelis came up with a novel design package. Unlike any of its major competitors, the engine and transmission are in the front of the vehicle. In this position the power pack adds its bulk to an already effective array of spaced armour. In fact all the components of the tank are arranged to increase crew protection. The suspension, even the diesel fuel storage cells, are arranged to absorb the impact of warheads before they can penetrate into the crew compartment. If any warhead does break through, there is a Spectronixs fire detection/extinguishing system. This uses Halon gas to minimise any chance of brewing up. In the 1982 Lebanon War although many Merkavas were damaged, none were destroyed. This despite numerous hits from Rocket Propelled Grenades (RPG's), tank rounds, and even sophisticated weaponry such as Milan and HOT. What is more important from the Israeli point of view, no crew member died. The rear doors offered an additional escape route with some degree of protection.

Merkava I early model.   *(Copyright of Marsh Gelbart)*

Merkava II, stationary side view, tank without side skirts, note running gear.
(Copyright of Marsh Gelbart)

All the ammunition is stored in special fire resistant containers positioned below the turret ring. This limits the prospect of a disastrous explosion should the armoured shell of the tank be penetrated.

On the original model Merkava there was a potentially dangerous shot trap at the rear of the turret bustle. The Israelis are not averse to adopting crude, ad hoc solutions to problems. A Heath Robinson device, consisting of weighted balls and chains, was fitted to the turret bustle. Its function is to explode the warheads of RPGs before they impact on the turret rear. This contraption was fitted originally to the Mark II tank and then retro-fitted to earlier Merkavas. The sophistication of the early model Merkava is evident in its clever layout rather than the elegance of its technology.

The Mark II machine, which came into service in 1983, introduced further improvements in protection which were retro-fitted to earlier models. The improvements included additional armour to the turret roof and special armour side skirts equipped with more resilient mountings.

FIREPOWER

The Merkava Mark I and II are armed with a M68 105mm cannon. With the use of advanced ammunition, the cannon proved effective against Syrian T-72s in the fighting in Lebanon in 1982. The ammunition in question consists of the M111 and M413 APDS tungsten rounds made by Israel Military Industries. These are considered at least the equal of similar NATO rounds. The rear hatch allows rapid resupply of ammunition in relative safety. The layout of the tank allows the storage of up to 92 cannon shells of 105mm rather than the average 50 or so found in most MBTs with a gun of the same calibre. An infantry squad of four men can be carried in some discomfort, if the ammunition load is removed from the

rear stowage space.

The cannon barrel is wrapped in a thermal shroud to improve accuracy. Because of careful design, it has proved relatively easy to up-gun the tank. The cannon is mounted in a large, wedge shaped turret. Despite its size, the turret when viewed from the business end has a very narrow profile. In fact the area visible to a potential enemy head on, is even smaller than that offered by the T-72 with its low, restricted turret. The only problem with the turret/gun assembly is that, because of the front mounted engine, the Merkava can only depress its main gun minus eight degrees. To take full advantage of firing from a hull down position, minus ten degrees would be preferable. The Merkava has the usual 7.62mm MG mounted coaxial to the main armament. It also carries two 7.62mm MGs on the turret roof along with a 60mm mortar and a 12.7mm MG mounted over the main gun barrel. The latter weapon was used to good effect as a supplement to the 105mm cannon in the urban fighting in Lebanon.

One problem on early model Merkavas, was that the gunner lacked thermal imaging. He had a good Laser range finder and digital computer, but he really needed better equipment for night fighting. Improvements in fire control were introduced with the arrival of the Mark II tank. It is likely that a thermal channel was retro-fitted to the fire control systems of early Merkavas as they underwent maintenance.

MOBILITY

Although the Merkava has excellent battlefield manoeuvrability, there is no disguising the fact that it is under-powered. Its engine (a super charged version of that used in the M-60), was meant for a machine 10 tons lighter. There is some gain – the changed centre of gravity with a front power-pack, means that the tank can get traction and haul its way up slopes of some 70%. Most of the Merkava's competitors can just manage gradients of 60%. The Mark II Merkava saw the fitting of an improved transmission, although the original engine was maintained.

ASSESSMENT

It is likely that the Merkava will be around for a while, although it probably won't turn up outside Israeli service. Early obsolescence was avoided, by designing the tank from the start with future upgrading in mind. Even the Mark I and II Merkavas which lack the advantage of advanced passive armour, are exceptionally well protected fighting machines. Any deficiencies in mobility and fire power have been largely negated in later models of the machine. All in all the Israelis have put into service an impressive MBT.

SERVICE STATUS
Merkava I and II are only in service with the Israeli Defence Forces. Approximately 600 are in service, all brought up to Mark II standard.

Prototype:	1977
In service:	MARK I 1979, MARK II 1983
Crew:	4
Armament:	Main, 105mm cannon. Secondary, coaxial 1 x 7.62mm MG, anti-aircraft 2 x 7.62mm MG. Additional, 1 x 12.7mm MG, 1 x 60mm Mortar
Combat weight:	63,000kg
Power-to-weight ratio:	14.28hp/t
Ground pressure:	0.9kg/cm^2
Length gun forward:	8.63m
Hull length:	7.45m
Hull width:	3.7m
Height (to commander's cupola):	2.75m
Ground clearance:	0.47m
Power pack:	TCM AVDS-1790-6A V-12 air-cooled turbo-charged diesel of 900hp coupled to an Allison transmission. The Mark II has an Israeli Ashot transmission
Max range (internal fuel):	400km
Fording (unprepared):	1.4m
Gradient:	70%
Side slope:	40%
Vertical obstacle:	0.95m

Trial vehicle for the Merkava. Built on Centurion hull to test front engined concept. *(Copyright of Marsh Gelbart)*

MANUFACTURER: ISRAELI ORDNANCE FACTORIES

BACKGROUND

Superficially resembling earlier Merkavas and sharing elements of their design, the Mark III is a much more advanced and formidable MBT. The Mark III maintains the front engined layout of its predecessors, and similarly focuses on survivability as the dominant design factor. However, thanks to innovative engineering, not only is the level of protection increased, but firepower and mobility are considerably improved.

PROTECTION

Merkava III was the first of the new generation of MBTs in service to have detachable, modular armour. The machine has a basic steel armour frame, upon which modules filled with special armour are attached. The modules – which contain armour comparable to Chobham – are fitted primarily to the front of the hull and the turret. Modular armour can be easily replaced if battle damaged. Additionally as new advanced armour becomes available, then the modules can be supplanted by higher performing variants. Approximately 50% of the armour package is modular in design. Thus the Merkava

III is relatively easy to patch up on the battlefield and to renovate and upgrade.

Protection of the tanks' sides is of an unusually high standard. The Merkava III has its sponsons and full length bazooka plates made of special armour. The bazooka plates have ingenious spring mounted attachments, these help prevent the plates being torn off when the tank moves through rough terrain. As in earlier Merkavas the Mark III's fuel cells add their mass to the tanks protective shell. External fuel cells at the rear of the tank, on either side of the vehicles rear hatch, are covered in high resistance armoured mesh.

A trio of external sensors – which give 360 degree coverage – warn the tank commander if the Merkava III has been illuminated by enemy targeting lasers. Smoke grenade dischargers each side of the turret would help screen the vehicle, if the threat indicators suggest that this is necessary.

The Mark III has an improved NBC system and carries a Spectronixs fire extinguishing system.

FIREPOWER

The Merkava III, unlike its predecessors, is equipped with a 120mm smooth bore cannon. This Israeli weapon

Merkava III on the Golan Heights.   *(Copyright of Marsh Gelbart)*

is similar to the commonly used German gun of the same calibre. The cannon can, if necessary, fire standard NATO ammunition as well as advanced rounds produced locally. The Merkava's weapon has a compact breech that makes the gun relatively easy to retro-fit into Mark I and II Merkavas (and indeed other, older MBTs), when they undergo upgrading. The tank carries at least 50 rounds of ammunition. Like earlier model Merkavas, ammunition can be loaded rapidly through the tanks rear doors and is stored in fire-proof containers below the level of the turret ring.

The fire control system of the latest Merkavas is excellent, comparing favourably with any other in service. It incorporates not only the usual laser range finders, meteorological sensors, and thermal imaging, found in any other top notch MBT, but also an automatic tracking system that locks on a designated target. This device improves chances of a first shot kill, even if both the Merkava and its intended prey are on the move.

Like earlier Merkavas the Mark III has the usual Israeli predilection for mounting up to four machine guns as secondary weaponry for use against infantry and to deter helicopters. Additionally a 60mm mortar, which can be fired from under armour, is mounted on the turret roof.

MOBILITY

The Merkava III boasts a more powerful supercharged engine than its predecessors (1,200hp against 908hp for earlier machines), but is still under-powered when compared with some of its main rivals. The Merkava III compensates for this by having an advanced coiled spring suspension. This incorporates not only a large range of vertical travel for the road wheels, but also effective hydraulic rotary dampers and bump stops. The combination gives considerable shock absorption and allows the Merkava to exploit its maximum cross country speed without shaking the crew to bits.

ASSESSMENT

Despite being slightly under-powered the Merkava III is amongst the top five MBTs in service. Future models of the Merkava are in the process of development, under the continuing incisive influence of General Tal. It is likely that the Merkava will remain one of the most formidable MBTs in service for many years to come.

SERVICE STATUS

Approximately 300 Merkava III tanks are in service, and numbers are increasing. At present it is only in service with the Israeli Defence Forces.

Merkava III crewman perched on the front of the tanks hull.

(Copyright of Marsh Gelbart)

Merkava III.

(Copyright of Marsh Gelbart)

Rear view of Merkava III showing ball and chain device to protect the shot trap at the turret rear, plus the rear access/ escape hatch, sandwiched between two external armoured fule cells.
(Copyright of Marsh Gelbart)

Merkava III. *(Copyright of Marsh Gelbart)*

Prototype:	1986
In service:	1989
Crew:	4
Armament:	Main, 120mm smooth bore cannon. Secondary, coaxial 1 x 7.62mm MG, anti-aircraft 2 x 7.62mm MG. Additional, 1 x 12.7mm MG, 1 x 60mm mortar
Combat weight:	62,000kg
Power-to-weight ratio:	19.35hp/t
Ground pressure:	0.96kg/cm^2
Length gun forward:	8.78m
Hull length:	7.6m
Hull width:	3.7m
Height (to commander's cupola):	2.76m
Ground clearance:	0.53m
Power pack:	TCM AVDS 1790-9AR V12 turbocharged diesel developing 1,200hp
Max road speed:	55km/h
Max range (internal fuel):	500km
Fording (unprepared):	1.38m
Gradient:	70%
Side slope:	40%
Vertical obstacle:	1m

MANUFACTURER: OTOBREDA

BACKGROUND

Built specifically for the export market, the OF-40 tank incorporates some components of the Leopard 1 and physically resembles the German tank. At present the tank has only been sold to the United Arab Emirates. Developed from 1977 and first built in 1980, the tank has ceased production, but the production line could be restarted if orders were forthcoming.

PROTECTION

The tank has an all-welded steel hull with a well-sloped glacis and turret front. An NBC system, smoke grenades and automatic fire extinguishing equipment are fitted as standard.

FIREPOWER

The tank carries a 105mm rifled cannon built by OTOBREDA. In total 57 rounds of ammunition for the main gun are stowed, 15 in the turret for ready use. Early models of the tank were fitted with digital fire control but not with a gun stabilisation system. Later production tanks, known as the OF-40 Mark 2, carry an improved fire control system. This incorporates gun stabilisation and input from meteorological sensors as standard. A projected development of the OF-40, the OF-40/120 Mk 2A offers a smoothbore 120mm cannon, mounted in a new turret based on that of the Ariete.

MOBILITY

The OF-40 carries a liquid cooled diesel that gives a decent power to weight ratio. Suspension is of the torsion bar type; of the seven road wheels on each side, five

OF-40 firing.   *(Courtesy of Will Fowler)*

OF-40 side view.   *(Courtesy of the Manufacturer)*

OF-40 paused at side of slope, three quarter front view.   *(Courtesy of Manufacturer)*

carry hydraulic shock absorbers. The projected OF-40/ 120 MK 2A would carry a more powerful engine of 1,000hp and have a better power to weight ratio.

ASSESSMENT

The tank is designed for the export market and within those constraints is a perfectly serviceable fighting vehicle. It has not sold particularly well, not because the tank has any inherent faults, but because purchasers tend to buy the latest and most complex MBT available that they can afford.

SERVICE STATUS

Only 36 tanks have been purchased to date and are used by Dubai.

Prototype:	1980
In service:	1981
Crew:	4
Armament:	Main, 105mm rifled cannon. Secondary, coaxial 1 x 7.62mm MG, anti-aircraft 1 x 7.62mm MG
Combat weight:	45,500kg
Power-to-weight ratio:	18.24hp/t
Ground pressure:	0.92kg/cm²
Length gun forward:	9.22m
Hull length:	6.89m
Hull width:	3.51m
Height (to turret roof):	2.45m
Ground clearance:	0.44m
Power pack:	MTU MB 838 Ca M-500 V-10, ten cylinder diesel of 830hp coupled to an automatic transmission
Max road speed:	60km/h
Max range (internal fuel):	600km
Fording (unprepared)):	1.2m
Gradient:	60%
Side slope:	30%
Vertical obstacle:	1.1m

MANUFACTURER: IVECO/OTOBREDA

BACKGROUND

Developed from 1984 to meet an Italian requirement for a Leopard 1 and M60 replacement, the C1 Ariete has been produced since 1993. The tank has the usual characteristics of any modern MBT, including composite armour, a 120mm gun and a high power to weight ratio. The present production run is for 200 vehicles.

PROTECTION

The C1 Ariete has a hull of all-welded steel construction. Composite armour has been added to the front of the hull and the front and side aspects of the turret. This gives the frontal arc of the tank increased protection. The running gear is protected by side skirts. The tank has the angular appearance typical of those protected by modern laminated armour.

The Ariete has stowage for 15 rounds of ammunition in the turret bustle. Blow off panels are fitted to the turret roof to vent any secondary explosions away from the crew should the tanks armoured shell be pierced.

The tank is fitted with a laser warning sensor, a modern NBC system and smoke grenades.

FIREPOWER

The tank has an Italian built 120mm smoothbore cannon that can fire NATO standard ammunition. In total, 42 rounds of 120mm ammunition are carried. A modern fire control system, known as the Officine Galileo TURMS, integrates a laser rangefinder, gunner's and commander's sights and a ballistic computer. The commander's sights incorporate a thermal imaging capability. Gun stabilisation, a thermal sleeve and meteorological sensors, all help to increase gun accuracy. The Ariete can engage moving targets whilst it itself is on the move.

MOBILITY

The Ariete has a high power to weight ratio thanks to a supercharged diesel. A German built automatic transmission assists in maximising efficiency. Suspension is torsion bar; there are seven road wheels on each side, five of which are fitted with hydraulic bumpers.

Ariete on the move.   *(Courtesy of Manufacturer)*

Ariete at rest.   *(Courtesy of Manufacturer)*

ASSESSMENT

The tank is modern and well equipped. However the Ariete has not yet reached its full potential. It is likely that the C1 Ariete will be replaced in production by the C2 Ariete which will have better protection, an autoloader and more powerful engine.

SERVICE STATUS

In service with the Italian Army. An initial batch of 200 is in the process of being delivered.

Prototype:	1986
In service:	1994
Crew:	4
Armament:	Main, 120mm smoothbore cannon. Secondary, 1 x 7.62mm MG, anti-aircraft 1 x 7.62mm MG
Combat weight:	54,000kg
Power-to-weight ratio:	24.7hp/t
Ground pressure:	0.85kg/cm^2
Length gun forward:	9.67m
Hull length:	7.59m
Hull width:	3.6m
Height (to turret roof):	2.5m
Ground clearance:	0.44m
Power pack:	IVECO V-12 MTCA turbocharged diesel of 1,300hp coupled to an automatic transmission
Max road speed:	65km/h
Max range:	550 to 600km
Fording (unprepared):	1.2m
Gradient:	60%
Side slope:	30%
Vertical obstacle:	2.1m

MANUFACTURER: MITSUBISHI HEAVY INDUSTRIES

BACKGROUND

The Type 61 was the first indigenous tank built in Japan after the Second World War. Development began in 1954, the first prototype was constructed in 1957 and the first Type 61 tank was accepted into service in 1962. Although supplanted by the later Type 74 and Type 90 models, the tank remains in service. The Type 61 was built bearing in mind the average difference in body size between American and Japanese servicemen. It was tailored to provide a better ergonomic fit than US supplied vehicles.

PROTECTION

The Type 61 has a welded steel hull with a cast turret. Since introduction into service, the tank has had smoke grenade dischargers installed. The ballistic shape of the tank is generally good, although there is a shot trap to the turret rear. The tank is lower and has a smaller battlefield signature than the comparable US M47.

FIREPOWER

The Type 61 has a turret similar to that of the American M47, fitted with a 90mm rifled cannon. Fire control is provided by a basic coincidence rangefinder and is assisted by an infra-red searchlight.

MOBILITY

The tank is fitted with a turbocharged diesel, an advanced engine when compared to the petrol fuelled powerpacks used by many of the tank's contemporaries. A torsion bar suspension with hydraulic shock absorbers is fitted.

ASSESSMENT

The Type 61 is a fairly basic tank and its capabilities reflect its vintage. It is roughly comparable to the US M47 in terms of capability.

SERVICE STATUS

In service only with the Japanese Army. Some 560 were produced, of which 190 remain in service.

Prototype:	1957
In service:	1962
Crew:	4
Armament:	Main, 90mm rifle cannon. Secondary, coaxial 1 x 7.62mm MG, anti-aircraft, 1 x 12.7mm MG
Combat weight:	35,000kg
Power-to-weight ratio:	17.14hp/t
Ground pressure:	0.95kg/cm^2
Length gun forward:	8.19m
Hull length:	6.3m
Hull width:	2.95m
Height (to turret roof):	2.49m
Ground clearance:	0.4m
Power pack:	Mitsubishi Type 12 Hm 21 WT V-12 turbocharged diesel of 600hp coupled to a mechanical transmission
Max road speed:	45km/h
Max range (Internal fuel):	200km
Fording (Unprepared):	0.9m
Gradient:	60%
Side slope:	30%
Vertical obstacle:	0.7m

Type 61 in the shadow of Mt Fuji.   *(Courtesy of Manufacturer)*

MANUFACTURER: MITSUBISHI HEAVY INDUSTRIES

BACKGROUND

This tank had an unusually long gestation period. The project began in 1962, when design requirements were drawn up, but the first production standard tanks were not built until 1975.

The Type 74 is a clear generation ahead of its predecessor. It shows distinct improvements, particularly in terms of its firepower and mobility.

PROTECTION

The tank has an all-welded steel hull and a cast steel turret. The turret in particular has an excellent ballistic shape. Upgrades to the tank in the late 1980s saw additional armour applied to the turret's frontal aspect including the roof.

FIREPOWER

The Type 74 mounts a 105mm rifled cannon based on the British L7 weapon. In recent years a thermal sleeve has been added. Some 55 rounds of 105mm ammunition are carried, 14 in the turret. Attempts at the tank's prototype stage to introduce an autoloader were abandoned as it proved too complex. The fire control system although more comprehensive than that of the Type 61 is fairly simple. A laser rangefinder is coupled to a rather basic ballistic computer for targeting purposes.

MOBILITY

The tanks most advanced feature is its suspension. The hydropneumatic suspension can be altered to regulate the height of the tank. This can be used to adjust the tanks ride to match different terrain. When the tank is stationary, the suspension can be used to provide a reduced battlefield signature by lowering the tanks hull. The suspension is also able to tilt the front of the tank upwards or downwards to give the main cannon increased angles of elevation and depression.

ASSESSMENT

The tank demonstrated some very interesting and advanced design features as far as its running gear is concerned. Protection and firepower were comparable to contemporary designs and certainly adequate to deal with any potential enemies. The tank is in service only

Type 74 at rest, front right view.   *(Courtesy of Manufacturer)*

Type 74 equipped with white light/infra red projector. *(Courtesy of John Norris)*

with the Japanese army. As with other Japanese tanks, a low production rate has made the tank very expensive. It is gradually being supplemented by the highly advanced Type 90.

SERVICE STATUS
In service with Japan, 870 tanks.

Prototype:	1969
In service:	1975
Crew:	4
Armament:	Main, 105mm rifled cannon. Secondary, coaxial 1 x 7.62mm MG, anti-aircraft 1 x 7.62mm MG
Combat weight:	38,000kg
Power-to-weight ratio:	18.94hp/t
Ground pressure:	0.86kg/cm²
Length gun forward:	9.42m
Hull length:	6.7m
Hull width:	3.18m
Height (to turret top):	2.48m (can be reduced by altering the suspension)
Ground clearance:	Adjustable from 0.2 to 0.65m
Power pack:	Mitsubishi 10ZF V-10 air cooled diesel of 720hp coupled to a manual transmission
Max road speed:	53km/h
Max range (internal fuel):	300km
Fording (unprepared):	1m
Gradient:	60%
Side slope:	40%
Vertical obstacle:	1m

MANUFACTURER: MITSUBISHI HEAVY INDUSTRIES

BACKGROUND
The Type 90 is the first Japanese tank to be at the cutting edge of technology, in several aspects of its design it is ahead of most of its competitors. Like other Japanese post-war tanks, the Type 90 had a long gestation. The design requirements date back to 1974, the first test bed (without turret), was completed in 1982, and the production standard tank was only available in 1992.

PROTECTION
The Type 90 is the first Japanese tank to use special laminated armour. The tank has the slab-sided, angular appearance typical of Chobham style protection. The design of the armour is indigenous; the armour is applied to the frontal arc of the tank, both hull and turret. A modern NBC system is carried. The Type 90 offers greatly increased protection when compared to previous Japanese MBTs.

The Type 90 has a self-defence suit, incorporating laser detectors that warn if the vehicle has been painted by enemy targeting lasers. The system is capable of launching smoke grenades and decoys to screen the tank and spoil an enemy's aim.

FIREPOWER
The tank mounts a licence built 120mm smoothbore cannon, based on the widely used German design. An autoloader is fitted in the turret bustle, with 16 rounds ready for immediate use. The bustle has blow-out panels to direct any ammunition explosion, away from the main body of the tank.

A particularly advanced and comprehensive fire control system is fitted to the Type 90. A laser rangefinder, thermal camera and a digital computer are all standard. The gunner and commander have linked sights and a sophisticated hunter/killer target tracker. The commander can find a target and lock on it. The target is automatically tracked even if it and the Type 90 are both on the move. The commander can either fire at the target himself, or designate the locked-on target to the gunner and search for further prey whilst the gunner engages the initial threat.

Type 90 in the snow.   *(Courtesy of John Norris)*

Type 90. *(Courtesy of Manufacturer)*

MOBILITY

The tank is equipped with a hybrid suspension incorporating features of both a torsion bar suspension and a hydropneumatic one. The middle pair of road wheels have a torsion bar suspension, the front and rear pair hydropneumatic suspension. The Type 90 can tilt its hull upwards or downwards. Because of this feature, it can bring its main armament to bear on targets at particularly awkward angles.

A powerful turbocharged diesel gives an exceptionally high power to weight ratio. Given the suspension and power pack, it is likely that the Type 90 has outstanding mobility.

ASSESSMENT

It may have taken a long time to get the beast in service, but the wait has been worth it. The tank has some exceptionally advanced features, in particular the hunter/killer fire control system. Any qualms about the tank relate to its slow rate of introduction into service, and the low rate of production which make makes the Type 90 very expensive.

SERVICE STATUS

About 100 of the Type 90 are in service with the Japanese Army. Introduction of further tanks continues at a slow pace.

Prototype:	1982
In service:	1992
Crew:	3
Armament:	Main, 120mm smoothbore cannon. Secondary, coaxial 1 x 7.62mm MG, anti-aircraft 1 x 12.7mm MG
Combat weight:	50,000kg
Power-to-weight ratio:	30hp/t
Ground pressure:	0.89kg/cm^2
Length gun forward:	9.76m
Hull length:	7.5m
Hull width:	3.43m
Height (to turret roof):	2.34m
Ground clearance:	0.45m is the norm, variable between 0.2 and 0.6m
Power pack:	Mitsubishi 10ZG 10-cylinder water cooled diesel of 1,500hp coupled to an automatic transmission
Max road speed:	70km/h
Max range (internal fuel):	350 to 400km
Fording (unprepared):	2m
Gradient:	60%
Side slope:	40%
Vertical obstacle:	1m

MANUFACTURER: HYUNDAI

BACKGROUND
The Type 88 tank, sometimes referred to as the K-1 or ROKIT, was designed for the Korean government by Chrysler Defence. Launched in 1980, the project led to a tank that was technically advanced, and which met specific design criteria requested by South Korea. The Type 88 incorporates some of the most advanced Western technology chosen to suit local operational requirements. Ergonomics are tailored to the average height of Korean crewmen.

Production of the tank, in three distinct batches, commenced in Korea in 1984. Some 833 vehicles were ordered and most have been delivered. A next generation Type 88 (the K-1A1), is under development.

PROTECTION
The hull and turret are welded steel, however efforts have been made to improve protection of the frontal arc of the tank. American manufactured Chobham armour, has been added to the front and sides of both hull and turret, this gives increased protection against HEAT and kinetic energy projectiles.

The tank is fitted with smoke grenades, NBC protection and an automatic fire detection/suppression system.

FIREPOWER
The tank mounts the American version of the British 105mm rifled cannon; ammunition is produced locally. Some 47 rounds are stowed for the main gun. The cannon is fitted with the usual fume extractor and thermal sleeve. It also has a muzzle reference system to maximise accuracy. The fire control system is comprehensive. It uses a ballistic computer built by CDC which has meteorological input from sensors mounted on the tank. The commander has a French built, stabilised, panoramic, day sight. The gunners day/night sights are similar to those used on the M1. The gunner has either a Stabilised Gunners Primary Sight built by Hughes, or a Texas Instruments Gunners Primary Tank Thermal Sight.

The Improved Type 88 is likely to be fitted with a 120mm smooth bore gun, and an improved fire control system.

MOBILITY
The tank has a high power to weight ratio thanks to a powerful 1,200 German diesel. An unusually complex, hybrid suspension is installed, with torsion bars for the middle two pairs of road wheels, and hydropneumatic suspension for the other four pairs of road wheels. The tank is able to depress its gun further using this feature.

ASSESSMENT
A useful fighting vehicle, the Type 88 melds together

Two views of Type 88 MBT. *(Courtesy of Military Attache South Korean Embassy)*

Korean operational requirements and advanced military technology from the West. The Improved Type 88 should be an even more formidable MBT.

SERVICE STATUS
In service with the Korean Army only. Approximately 800 out of 833 ordered are in service.

Type 88 fords obstacle. *(Courtesy of Military Attache South Korean Embassy)*

Prototype:	1983
In service:	1985
Crew:	4
Armament:	Main, 105mm rifled cannon. Secondary, coaxial 1 x 7.62mm MG, anti-aircraft 1 x 12.7mm MG & 1 x 7.62mm MG
Combat weight:	51,000kg
Power-to-weight ratio:	23.5hp/t
Ground pressure:	0.86kg/cm^2
Length gun forward:	9.67m
Hull length:	7.477m
Hull width:	3.59m
Height (to turret top):	2.25m
Ground clearance:	0.46m
Power pack:	MTU M8 871 Ka-501 V-8 diesel of 1,200hp, coupled to an automatic transmission
Max road speed:	65km/h
Max range (internal fuel):	500km
Fording (unprepared):	1.2m
Gradient:	60%
Side slope:	40%
Vertical obstacle:	1m

MANUFACTURER: PAKISTANI STATE ORDNANCE FACTORIES

BACKGROUND

The MBT 2000, also known as the Al-Khalid, is a Pakistani development, but one that relies heavily on Chinese technology and design skills. Pakistani industry sensibly built up its manufacturing capabilities in incremental stages. Expertise in upgrading older Chinese tanks such as the Type 59, was gradually supplemented by the capability to assemble and co-produce more sophisticated MBTs. Design features from these later machines, the Type 69-II and Type 85-II, are thought to be carried over to the MBT 2000.

The project to produce an indigenous tank – albeit one that owed much to Chinese MBTs – was launched in 1988. The first prototype was built in 1991. Unspecified problems have slowed down the development of the MBT 2000, and it is not yet in service.

PROTECTION

The tank has an all-welded steel hull and turret. A layer of laminated composite armour is added to the tanks frontal arc. The appliqué composite armour has been designed in an easily removable and replaceable modular format. New modules can be fitted either to replace battle damage or to introduce superior levels of protection as new armour materials become available. At the users request, bricks of reactive armour can be fitted to the tanks vulnerable portions, increasing the tank's level of protection. Side skirts with a wavy profile are fitted as standard.

An NBC system and smoke grenades are installed on the prototype.

FIREPOWER

The tank mounts a fully stabilised, smoothbore, 125mm cannon with associated autoloader. The gun has a thermal sleeve and fume extractor. A modern fire control system with day/night sights, environmental sensors, and digital computer is thought to be fitted. An ability to engage moving targets is probable. The origin of the fire control system is unknown, but it is likely to have come from a Western European manufacturer.

MOBILITY

A diesel engine of 1,200hp is fitted to prototypes; production vehicles are intended to have 1,500hp diesels. Even with the earlier power pack, the MBT 2000 has a very good power to weight ratio and is likely to be an agile fighting machine. The diesel engine being trialled by the prototype, is thought to be the same Perkins diesel as fitted to Challenger, coupled to the automatic transmission used by the Leclerc. Torsion bar suspension is fitted to the MBT 2000.

ASSESSMENT

If Pakistan can overcome the difficulties inherent in launching into such an ambitious project as the MBT 2000, then the tank is likely to be an impressive fighting machine.

SERVICE STATUS

Not yet in service.

(Provisional)

Prototype:	1991
In service:	Not yet in service
Crew:	3
Armament:	Main, 125mm smoothbore cannon. Secondary, coaxial 1 x 7.62mm MG, anti-aircraft 1 x 12. 7mm MG
Combat weight:	48,000kg
Power-to-weight ratio:	25hp/t
Hull length:	6.9m
Hull width:	3.4m
Height (to turret top):	2.3m
Power pack:	Perkins Engines CV-12 diesel of 1,200hp coupled to an automatic transmission
Max road speed:	62km/h
Max range (internal fuel):	400km
Gradient:	60%
Side slope:	40%
Vertical obstacle:	0.85m

MANUFACTURER: ZAKLADY MECHANICZNE
BUMAR-LABEDY SA

BACKGROUND

Poland had long produced Soviet designs under licence, often building the machines to a high standard of quality control and adding local modifications. The T-72 M1 MBT in service with Poland and Iran is a recent example. With the PT-91 Twardy, Polish industry has taken one step further. They have constructed a tank, which although based on the T-72, is sufficiently different to warrant consideration as a separate MBT. Improved components as fitted to the Twardy can also be retrofitted to basic T-72s. The Twardy completed successful trials with the Polish army in 1995 and delivery of vehicles for full scale service is imminent.

PROTECTION

The Twardy has the basic protection levels of the late model T-72, with the addition of Polish explosive reactive armour added to its hull and turret. The reactive armour is known as ERAWA-1. (More sophisticated reactive armour with two layers of explosive, ERAWA-2, has also been produced. The latter is capable of disrupting modern, tandem warhead, HEAT rounds). The tank's steel side skirts are also fitted with reactive armour modules over the front three pairs of road wheels.

The tank has four laser warning sensors that alert the crew if the vehicle has been painted by targeting lasers. If that does occur, then the Twardy is fitted with an extensive array of smoke grenade launchers, 12 on each side of the turret. Efforts have also been made to reduce the electronic signature of the tank by the selective use of radar absorbent paint.

An improved NBC system and fire detection/ suppression equipment have been fitted. Additional efforts to maximise crew survivability include better protection for the driver's seat should the tank detonate a mine, and if the worst comes to the worst, an escape hatch in the tank's belly.

FIREPOWER

The 125mm smoothbore gun, complete with autoloader, is that of the T-72 MBT series. The gun is fully stabilised.

PT-91 with a clear view of its close fitting modules of explosive reactive armour.   *(Courtesy of the Manufacturer)*

Gun laying has been modernised. A new digital fire control computer is installed, a laser rangefinder is standard, and an Israeli thermal sight, built by EL-OP, equips the gunner. The tank is equipped to mount the Polish designed PW-LWD rocket-propelled mine-breaching apparatus.

MOBILITY
The tank has a similar power to weight ratio when compared to the T-72, despite a growth in weight. This is the result of the standard power pack being up-rated from 769 to 850hp. The suspension system is unchanged. Improved tracks – incorporating rubber pads – have helped reduced noise and maintenance times. Enlarged fuel capacity has increased road range to 650km.

ASSESSMENT
The Twardy represents an evolutionary improvement over the T-72, however it is operating in a crowded market niche and faces fierce competition from the Russian T-80 and Ukrainian T-84. At present, Polish industry is working on the Goryl (Gorilla) MBT, a further development of the Twardy. The Goryl will represent a substantial advance in Polish armoured vehicle construction. The Goryl has a new turret which will incorporate advanced, second generation reactive armour. The Goryl also will have the ability to fire missiles from its 125mm smoothbore cannon.

SERVICE STATUS
Entry into service with the Polish Army is imminent.

Prototype:	1992
In service:	1996
Crew:	3
Armament:	Main, 125mm smoothbore cannon. Secondary, coaxial 1 x 7.62mm MG, anti-aircraft 1 x 12.7mm MG
Combat weight:	45,300kg
Power-to-weight ratio:	18.49hp/t
Ground pressure:	0.8kg/cm^2
Length gun forward:	9.53m
Hull length:	6.95m
Hull width:	3.59m
Height (to top of turret):	2.19m
Ground clearance:	0.395m
Power pack:	Type S-12U multi-fuel, supercharged water cooled diesel of 850hp coupled to an automatic transmission
Max road speed:	60km/h
Max range:	650km
Fording (with preparation): 5m using a snorkel	
Gradient:	60%
Side slope:	40%
Vertical obstacle:	0.85m

MANUFACTURER: ROMTEHNICA

BACKGROUND

Information about Romanian tank production is sketchy. The State owned company which manufactures Romanian tanks appears to have successfully re-designed the Russian T-55 greatly improving its fighting qualities. The TR-85 was first observed in 1977, whilst the TM-800, an up-rated export version of the TR-85, was announced in 1994. Both machines share elements of the earlier Romanian TR-580, the first Romanian upgrade of the T-55, including a lengthened hull with six pairs of road wheels. The increase in hull length was undertaken to facilitate the installation of a more powerful engine. The extra horsepower allows additional armour to be carried.

PROTECTION

Both the TR-85 and the TM-800 are substantially heavier than the T-55. The TR-85 weighs in at approximately 43,300kg, the TM-800 45,000kg, in comparison the basic T-55 weighs 36,000kg. Whilst some of the weight gain is accounted for by the longer hulls of the Romanian tanks, most of the additional tonnage is as a result of extra armour. In the case of the TM-800, laminated special armour is incorporated in both the hull and turret. This is expected to considerably improve survivability on the battlefield. Both tanks have sheet steel side-skirts. These would detonate HEAT projectiles and offer a degree of protection to the running gear.

The TM-800 has an anti-radiation liner for the crew compartment and an NBC system. It also carries smoke grenade launchers.

FIREPOWER

Both tanks carry a 100mm cannon, possibly of Russian or Chinese origin. The TM-800 has a ballistic computer and associated fire control system including a laser rangefinder, for its fully stabilised weapon The TR-85 has an externally mounted laser rangefinder above the gun mantelet.

MOBILITY

Despite their greater weight, both the Romanian MBTs have more powerful engines than the T-55 and thus correspondingly better power to weight ratios. The TR-85 is thought to have an engine of 600hp. For the TM-800 estimates vary widely from 620 to 830 hp.

ASSESSMENT

The T-55, a well established if obsolete design, has been comprehensibly modified to produce a more effective fighting machine. The advantage for potential users of the Romanian tanks is that the armed forces of states familiar with the T-55 would have no problem in converting to the TR-85 or TM-800. Some of the improvements standard on the Romanian machines are also being offered in kit form for retrofitting to T-54/55 series tanks.

SERVICE STATUS

Some 620 TR-85 tanks are in Romanian service. An unknown number are thought to be in service with Iraq.

(TM-800)	
Prototype:	Unknown
In service:	Unknown
Crew:	4
Armament:	Main, 100mm rifled cannon. Secondary, 1 x 7.62mm MG, anti-aircraft 1 x 12.7mm MG
Combat weight:	45,000kg
Power-to-weight ratio:	Unknown
Ground pressure:	0.895kg/cm^2
Length gun forward:	9.25m
Hull length:	6.74m
Hull width:	3.3m
Height (to turret top):	2.35m
Ground clearance:	0.43m
Power pack:	A diesel of unknown origin of approximately 620-830hp coupled to a manual transmission
Max road speed:	65km/h
Max range (internal fuel):	500km
Fording (unprepared):	1.4m
Gradient:	60%
Side slope:	40%
Vertical obstacle:	0.9m

MANUFACTURER: ROMTEHNICA

BACKGROUND

The TR-125 is based on the Russian T-72 tank, but as in the case of other Romanian produced tanks, there are significant improvements. The TR-125 has an extra pair of road wheels when compared with the T-72, is substantially heavier thanks to extra armour protection, and has a more powerful engine. Details of the TR-125 are frustratingly limited. Revealed in 1989, the tank is in limited production.

PROTECTION

The tank weighs 7,000kg more than the baseline T-72. Whilst some of the additional weight is undoubtedly due to increased length, much is as a result of additional armour. It is likely that the extra armour is concentrated on the portion of the tank most exposed to battle damage, i.e. the frontal arc of the turret and hull. The exact nature of the armour is unknown, but it is probably passive and made up of some form of laminated material. The side skirt of the TR-125 is different in appearance from that of the T-72. The smoke grenade array is also of a different design and appears to be particularly large. It is assumed that the NBC system is similar to that of the T-72.

FIREPOWER

The tank appears to carry the same weapon, and presumably the same autoloader as the T-72. Exact information on the fire control system is unavailable. The 125mm smoothbore cannon alleviates the main shortcoming of previous Romanian MBTs, their lack of a hard hitting punch.

MOBILITY

As the vehicle has a more powerful engine than the T-72, it has a better power to weight ratio, despite its greater weight when compared to the Russian machine.

ASSESSMENT

With the limited information available, it appears that the Romanians have produced a fighting vehicle that retains the good qualities of the T-72 plus some significant advantages. The TR-125's extra armour, and the more powerful engine, are noteworthy.

SERVICE STATUS

The TR-125 may have entered into service on a small scale with the Romanian army.

Prototype:	Unknown
In service:	Unknown
Crew:	3
Armament:	Main, 125mm smoothbore cannon. Secondary, 1 x 7.62mm MG, anti-aircraft 1 x 12.7mm MG
Combat weight:	48,000kg
Power-to-weight ratio:	18.33hp/t
Ground pressure:	Unknown
Length gun forward:	Unknown
Hull length:	Unknown
Hull width:	Unknown
Height (to commander's cupola):	Unknown
Ground clearance:	Unknown
Power pack:	880hp diesel
Max road speed:	60 to 65km/h
Max range (internal fuel):	350-400km
Fording (unprepared):	1.4m
Gradient:	60%
Side slope:	40%
Vertical obstacle:	0.9m

Since 1945, Russian tanks have in general been evolutionary designs, simple, robust and soldier proof. There has been one constant theme to Soviet (and CIS) tank design: to maintain a compact size and low silhouette. Despite a steady growth in gun calibre and engine power, the Russians have managed to keep the overall size of their successive tank designs within tight limits. They have done so partly through the installation of autoloaders. This has allowed them to reduce their crew requirements to three per tank.

The compact size of Russian tanks has led to serious drawbacks. Firstly and most importantly, the low profiles of Russian tanks has meant an inability to depress their main cannon beyond minus five degrees. This means that they can't fire effectively from hull down positions, without having to expose much of their turret and hull in bringing their cannon to bear. In other words by attempting to keep a low silhouette, the Russians afflicted their tanks with too prominent a tactical height.

Secondly the tanks have very cramped crew compartments, ergonomics are poor and crews exhaust easily.

Thirdly, the limited amount of stowage space means that shells are stowed above the turret ring, with all the risks that entails of catastrophic explosion should the turret should be pierced.

There are other fundamental short comings of Russian tanks apart from their cramped size. Although Russian tanks have generally thick armour and good ballistic shapes, they were slow to incorporate modern compound armour. Also whilst Russian tanks have since 1945 tended to carry weapons slightly larger than that of their Western competitors, they have lagged behind in the sophistication of both their ammunition and of fire control.

Despite all these shortcomings Russian designers should not be underestimated. They have fitted many of their tanks to fire cannon launched anti-tank missiles, thus increasing the lethality of their tanks. In addition it would not be surprising if the CIS were the first to field an MBT armed with a gun mounted in an external pod rather than a manned turret.

MANUFACTURER: Ex SOVIET UNION, CZECHOSLOVAKIA, POLAND

BACKGROUND

Possibly the best Second World War tank, despite the crude quality of its manufacture. Certainly the one that best blended protection, firepower and mobility in the same package. The versatile T-34 can be considered the first genuine MBT. The original T-34 armed with a 76mm cannon was produced in 1940. The improved T-34-85 armed with a more powerful 85mm cannon arrived on the scene in 1943. The T-34 is long obsolete.

PROTECTION

For the time of its manufacture the tank had excellent protection. Its thick, well-sloped armour set the trend for later MBTs. Although the basic design concept remains sound, the T-34-85's armour protection has been left behind by the firepower of modern MBTs. It also lacks NBC protection. The T-34-85 is vulnerable on the modern battlefield.

FIREPOWER

By the standards of World War Two the T-34 was well armed for a tank of its weight. The tank's fighting qualities were limited by poor ergonomics and rudimentary fire controls. Against a modern opponent the T-34-85 is outclassed. However the 85mm cannon should give pause for thought for any fighting vehicle other than a MBT.

MOBILITY

A good power to weight ratio and wide tracks gave the T-34-85 unsurpassed tactical mobility for its time. It retained excellent mobility in difficult terrain including desert and snowy steppes. The T-34-85 could also function in severe weather conditions, when German tanks were frozen static. Although obsolete, the tank's mobility remains impressive.

ASSESSMENT

A great tank in its day, the T-34-85 is no longer a first line weapon. However in the hands of minor armies

involved in bush wars, the T-34-85 can still be effective. The T-34-85 is most likely to be found in the field in Africa or in Asia.

SERVICE STATUS

Still present in the inventories of armies and insurgents in some thirty countries. For the most part, it is found in second line service or is moth-balled.

Prototype:	1943
In service:	1943
Crew:	5
Armament:	Main, 85mm cannon. Secondary, coaxial 1 x 7.62mm MG, bow, 1 x 7.62mm MG
Combat weight:	32,000kg
Power-to-weight ratio:	15.62hp/t
Ground pressure:	0.83kg/cm²
Length gun forward:	8.08m
Hull length:	6.19m
Hull width:	3.0m
Height:	2.74m
Ground clearance:	0.38m
Power pack:	V-2-34 or 34M V-12 diesel of 500hp
Max road speed:	55km/h
Max range:	300km
Fording (unprepared):	1.3m
Gradient:	60%
Side slope:	40%
Vertical obstacle:	0.73m

T-34/85 note spiked gun barrel. *(Copyright of Marsh Gelbart)*

MANUFACTURER: SOVIET MILITARY INDUSTRIES

BACKGROUND

The Soviet Union brought into service an interim replacement for the T-34 in 1944. This tank was known as the T-44; it proved unreliable and was supplanted in production by the T-54 in 1947. Manufacture of the T-54 continued until superseded by the T-55 in 1959. Produced in vast numbers, and with many variants, by the USSR, Poland and Czechoslovakia, the T-54 has had mixed success in combat.

PROTECTION

The T-54 has a well-shaped welded hull and a cast turret, the mushroom shaped profile of which enhances ballistic protection. The small size and low visual signature of the tank aid its battlefield survivability. The low signature is bought at the cost of poor human engineering. The cramped conditions within the fighting compartment limit crew effectiveness.

FIREPOWER

The tank was fitted with the 100mm D-10 cannon, a good gun but one that was outclassed by the widely used British 105mm L7 cannon. In recent years improved fire control, incorporating laser rangefinding, has been offered on the market. The laser usually being mounted externally above the gun mantelet.

The main problem with the T-54's firepower, and incidentally that of successive Soviet tanks, was its limited ability to depress its main gun. The T-54 can only depress its gun a mere minus four degrees compared to an average of minus ten for Western tanks. This prevents it from fighting effectively from hull-down positions.

The lack of gun stabilisation on early models of the tank, compounded by the absence a revolving turret floor, hampered the gun crew's best efforts.

MOBILITY

The mobility of the tank was good. On a strategic level its light weight allowed relatively easy movement by rail. Operationally the T-54's low battle mass allowed it to use bridges that other MBTs could not. Low ground pressure, a good starting system for cold weather, and a snorkel for river crossings, allowed mobility in difficult terrain.

Damaged Egyptian T-54 captured by the Israelis. Note this vehicle has been hit by 14 APDS rounds and 1 HEAT round.

(Copyright of Marsh Gelbart)

ASSESSMENT

Crude, uncomplicated and robust, the T-54 was a soldier-proof fighting machine. The tank had its battlefield failings and these were exposed by more sophisticated opponents.

SERVICE STATUS (T-54/55 family.)

The T54/55 family is still in widespread usage by up to 50 government armies or militia forces. However it is now obsolete and not found in the active inventories of leading armies. In service with; Afghanistan, 700 tanks. Albania has 721 Type 59 clones of the T-55 plus 15 actual T-55s. Algeria, 330 tanks. Angola, 100 tanks. Bangladesh, 60 tanks. Bulgaria, 1,276 tanks. Cambodia, 150 tanks including some Type 59 models. Central African Republic, 4 tanks. CIS, 8,000 tanks. Congo, 25 tanks. Croatia, 140 tanks. Cuba, 1,100 tanks. Czech Republic, 469 tanks. Egypt, 840 tanks. Ethiopia, 350 tanks. Finland, 70 tanks. Guinea, 8 tanks. Hungary, 873 tanks. India, 500 tanks. Iran, 110 tanks. Iraq, 500 tanks including Type 59 variants. Israel 300 tanks, most converted to TI-67 standard. Korea, North, 1,600 tanks. Laos, 30 tanks. Lebanon, 200 tanks. Libya, 1,600 tanks. Mali, 25 tanks. Mongolia, 650 tanks. Mozambique, 80 tanks. Nicaragua, 130 tanks, some in store. Nigeria, 60 tanks. Pakistan, 50 tanks. Peru, 300 tanks. Poland, 1,035 tanks. Romania, 822 tanks. Slovakia, 600 tanks. Slovenia, 40 tanks. Somalia, 100 tanks, probably none serviceable. Sri Lanka, 25 tanks. Sudan, 250 tanks. Syria 2,100 tanks, some in storage. Tanzania, 35 tanks, non-operational. Togo, 2 tanks. Vietnam, several hundred. Yemen, 675 tanks. Yugoslavia (Serbia/Montenegro), 407 tanks. Zambia, 10 tanks. Zimbabwe 40 tanks including Type 59 variants.

Prototype:	1946
In service:	1949
Crew:	4
Armament:	Main, 100mm cannon. Secondary, coaxial 1 x 7.62mm MG, bow, 1x 7.62mm MG, anti-aircraft 1 x 12.7mm MG
Combat weight:	36,000kg
Power-to-weight ratio:	14.44hp/t
Ground pressure:	0.81kg
Length gun forward:	9m
Hull length:	6.04m
Hull width:	3.27m
Height (to commander's cupola):	2.4m
Ground clearance:	0.43m
Power pack:	V-54 V-12 liquid cooled diesel of 520hp coupled to a manual transmission
Max road speed:	50km/h
Max range (internal fuel):	510km, on the road
Fording (unprepared):	1.4m
Gradient:	60%
Side slope:	40%
Vertical obstacle:	0.8m

T-54 side shot.   *(Courtesy of the Tank Museum)*

MANUFACTURER: SOVIET MILITARY INDUSTRIES

BACKGROUND

The T-55, first demonstrated on parade in 1961, probably made its initial entry into service in 1959. For all practical purposes the T-55 is an improved T-54. The majority of the upgrading was internal. There were few external differences other than the removal of a dome shaped vent forward of the loader's hatch.

PROTECTION

Unlike the baseline T-54, the T-55 was fitted from the onset with NBC protection. As later marks came into service, some rudimentary protection from radiation was installed, this took the form of foam backed, lead panels.

Late model T-55s are fitted with either reactive armour modules or passive armour upgrades to improve survivability. The widely used T-55AM, has a horseshoe shaped array of spaced armour for its turret.

FIREPOWER

The T-55 retained its predecessor's 100mm gun, however it improved gunnery performance by installing a partial, rotating turret basket floor. This reduced the loaders work load. As in the late model T-54, the cannon was stabilised in two planes, although the tank could only realistically fire with any kind of accuracy when stationary. The T-55 can carry nine more cannon rounds than its predecessor as it has abandoned the bow machine gun.

Late model T-55s have considerably more lethal firepower. Variants such as the T-55M can carry the 5,000 metre range Bastion (NATO designation AT-10 Stabber), a laser beam-riding missile, which can be launched from the tank's gun tube. Upgraded fire control systems are fitted along with the Bastion missile system.

MOBILITY

Compared to the T-54, the T-55 has a more powerful engine, a better power to weight ratio and thus greater mobility.

ASSESSMENT

Obsolete and simple to operate, the T-55 was until recently merely regarded as a "War Lord Special", i.e. a cheap, widely available tank ideal for low technology

T-55 side view.

wars. However the fitting of Bastion missiles means that retro-fitted T-55s need to be treated with respect. The T-54/55 family, in service with some 50 countries, remains one of the most widely disseminated armoured fighting vehicles in service. The combined production figures for the two tanks are well over 50,000 vehicles.

SERVICE STATUS (T-54 and T-55 family)

In service with, Afghanistan, 700 tanks. Albania has 721 Type 59 clones of the T-55 plus 15 actual T-55s. Algeria, 330 tanks. Angola, 100 tanks. Bangladesh, 60 tanks. Bulgaria, 1,276 tanks. Cambodia, 150 tanks including some Type 59 models. Central African Republic, 4 tanks. CIS, 8,000 tanks. Congo, 25 tanks. Croatia, 140 tanks. Cuba, 1,100 tanks. Czech Republic, 469 tanks. Egypt, 840 tanks. Ethiopia, 350 tanks. Finland, 70 tanks. Guinea, 8 tanks. Hungary, 873 tanks. India, 500 tanks. Iran, 110 tanks. Iraq, 500 tanks including Type 59 variants. Israel 300 tanks, most converted to TI-67 standard. Korea, North, 1,600 tanks. Laos, 30 tanks. Lebanon, 200 tanks. Libya, 1,600 tanks. Mali, 25 tanks. Mongolia, 650 tanks. Mozambique, 80 tanks. Nicaragua, 130 tanks, some in store. Nigeria, 60 tanks. Pakistan, 50 tanks. Peru, 300 tanks. Poland, 1,035 tanks. Romania, 822 tanks. Slovakia, 600 tanks. Slovenia, 40 tanks. Somalia, 100 tanks, probably none serviceable. Sri Lanka, 25 tanks. Sudan, 250 tanks. Syria 2,100 tanks, some in storage. Tanzania, 35 tanks, non-operational. Togo, 2 tanks. Vietnam, several hundred. Yemen, 675 tanks. Yugoslavia (Serbia/Montenegro), 407 tanks. Zambia, 10 tanks. Zimbabwe 40 tanks including Type 59 variants.

Prototype:	1958
In service:	1959
Crew:	4
Armament:	Main, 100mm cannon. Secondary, coaxial 1 x 7.62mm MG, anti-aircraft, 1 x 12.7mm MG
Combat weight:	36,000kg
Power-to-weight ratio:	16.11hp/t
Ground pressure:	0.81kg
Length gun forward:	9m
Hull length:	6.45m
Hull width:	3.27m
Height (to commander's cupola):	2.4m
Ground clearance:	0.43m
Power pack:	V-12 water cooled diesel of 580hp with a manual transmission
Max road speed:	48km/h
Max range (internal fuel):	460km on the road
Fording (unprepared):	1.4m
Gradient:	60%
Side slope:	40%
Vertical obstacle:	0.8m

MANUFACTURER: SOVIET MILITARY INDUSTRIES

BACKGROUND

It became clear that the 100mm gun of the T-54/55 was ineffective at the expected battle ranges of 1,000 metres, when compared to the British 105mm L7. Introduced in 1961, the T-62 was the Soviet response. The T-62 is marginally longer, wider and heavier than the T-55. The increase is that necessary to incorporate the more powerful 115mm smoothbore gun carried by the T-62.

PROTECTION

Substantially the same level of protection as the T-55. As with the earlier tank, later models of the T-62 have been retrofitted with a variety of reactive and passive armour.

FIREPOWER

The major change is of course the smoothbore 115mm weapon. When firing armour piercing, fin stabilised, discarding sabot ammunition, the cannon has a killing range of 1,600 metres. Although the turret had a marginal increase in size, the larger weapon makes the fighting compartment even more restrictive and claustrophobic. In an attempt to assist the loader, an automatic shell ejection system was fitted. Unfortunately this slowed up the firing cycle and often malfunctioned, hurling hot shell cases into the fighting compartment.

Initial fire control systems, sights and optics were basic. Like the T-55, the T-62 can be fitted with enhanced fire control systems incorporating laser rangefinders. The T-62 can be equipped to fire missiles from its gun tube. In this case a modified Bastion (A-10 Stabber) with a range of 5,000 metres.

MOBILITY

The vehicle uses the same torsion bar suspension system as the T-55 but has different spacing of its road wheels. The vehicle carries the same engine as the T-55, but it carries 4,000kg of extra weight.

ASSESSMENT

The T-62 really never replaced the T-55. Although its firepower was superior to its earlier stablemate, it carried

T-62 being put through its paces at the US Aberdeen Proving Ground.   *(Courtesy of Will Fowler)*

too much gun for so lightweight a tank. The poor ergonomics of the T-55 were made worse. This helps to explain the tanks indifferent combat record.

SERVICE STATUS

Afghanistan has 170 tanks in service. Algeria, 300 tanks. Angola, 100 tanks, serviceability unknown. Cuba, 400 tanks. Egypt, 500 tanks. Ethiopia, 100 tanks approximately. Iran 150 tanks. Iraq, 400 tanks. Israel, 110 tanks. Korea, North, 1,800 tanks. Libya, 350 tanks. Mongolia, unknown. Russia, 762 tanks, plus many more in storage east of the Urals. Syria, 1,000 tanks. Ukraine, 85 tanks. Vietnam, 200 tanks. Yemen, 150 tanks.

T-62 front right view. *(Copyright of Marsh Gelbart)*

T-62 captured by the Israelis and modified with external panniers to provide extra storage space and change the vehicles profile. *(Copyright of Marsh Gelbart)*

Prototype:	1958
In service:	1961
Crew:	4
Armament:	Main 115mm smoothbore cannon. Secondary, coaxial 1 x 7.62mm MG, anti-aircraft 1 x 12.7mm MG
Combat weight:	40,000kg,
Power-to-weight ratio:	14.5hp/t
Ground pressure:	0.77kg/cm²
Length gun forward:	9.34m
Hull length:	6.63m
Hull width:	3.3m
Height (including anti-aircraft gun):	2.4m
Ground clearance:	0.43m
Power pack:	V-55-5V liquid cooled diesel of 580hp coupled to a manual transmission
Max road speed:	50km/h
Max range (internal fuel):	450km on the road
Fording (unprepared):	1.4m
Gradient:	60%
Side slope:	30%
Vertical obstacle:	0.8m

MANUFACTURER: SOVIET MILITARY INDUSTRIES

BACKGROUND

The T-64 is a landmark in Soviet post-war tank construction. Unlike the usual evolutionary Soviet design process, the T-64 was a high risk project. It has new armour arrays, a new gun equipped with an autoloader, and an advanced power pack and suspension. The price for this adventurous approach is a decline in the tank's reliability, maintainability and availability.

PROTECTION

The T-64 pioneered the use of laminated armour in Soviet tanks. Although much of the armour protection is of steel, special armour panels incorporating ceramic materials are used on the T-64's hull and turret. "Gill" side skirts, sections of which angle away from the hull, offer better stand-off protection against HEAT rounds.

Some shadow of doubt hangs over the armour protection of the T-64. Late models of the tank such as the T-64BV, have reactive armour modules. This perhaps indicates that the original special laminates were not as effective as the Chobham type armour used in the West.

FIREPOWER

Early versions of the T-64 used the same weapon as the T-62. However the T-64 soon adopted the more powerful 125mm smoothbore cannon. The use of an automatic loader allows the crew to be reduced to three (commander, gunner and driver) and permits up to six rounds a minute to be fired. A rotating carousel holds 24 ready to use projectiles. If the autoloader malfunctions, then the cramped space makes manual loading especially awkward.

Fire control was initially rather old fashioned, using, coincidence rangefinding. It improved with the arrival of the T-64B which introduced a laser rangefinder. Later models such as the T-64B can fire the radio guided AT-8 Songster missile through the barrel of its 125mm gun. The T-64 generally carries six Songsters, with its range of 4,000 metres, and thirty-six standard shells, the latter have separate propellant charges.

MOBILITY

The T-64 is equipped with a new multi-fuel engine and an automatic transmission, the former more powerful and the latter more complex than previous efforts. The

T-64 from the front showing its explosive reactive modules to good advantage.   *(Courtesy of the Tank Museum)*

road wheels are smaller than is the norm with Soviet equipment, and the suspension more complicated, using as it does, additional hydraulic shock absorbers. It is thought that the new suspension and transmission, can prove especially troublesome, requiring constant repair and maintenance.

ASSESSMENT

A high risk venture relying on innovation rather than evolution. The T-64 did not quite succeed as it had too many untried components in one vehicle. It remains a formidable tank. In the 1980s the backbone of Soviet armour was made up of T-64s. Some 8,000 of the tank were produced. The T-64 was never exported for a combination of reasons, including: 1) The danger of too much advanced technology falling into the wrong hands, 2) The difficulty in maintaining the tank, and 3) Its expense.

SERVICE STATUS

In service with Russia, 625 tanks, plus others in storage. Ukraine, 2,345 tanks.

Prototype:	1961 Basic T-64
In service:	1967, Basic T-64 (T-64B in service 1984)
Crew:	3
Armament:	Main, 125mm smoothbore cannon. Secondary, 1 x 7.62mm MG, anti-aircraft, 1 x 12.7mm MG
Combat weight:	39,500kg (including 1,500kg of reactive armour)
Power-to-weight ratio:	17.7hp/t,(if reactive armour is fitted)
Ground pressure:	0.86kg/cm²
Length gun forward:	9.2m
Hull length:	6.35m
Hull width:	4.75m (with skirts)
Height (to commander's cupola):	2.2m
Ground clearance:	0.38m
Power pack:	5DTF-5 Cylinder opposed piston, liquid-cooled diesel of 700hp with synchromesh hydraulically assisted transmission
Max road speed:	75km
Max range (internal fuel):	400km
Fording (unprepared):	1.4m
Gradient:	60%
Side slope:	40%
Vertical obstacle:	0.8m

MANUFACTURER: SOVIET MILITARY INDUSTRIES

BACKGROUND

If the T-64 was an innovative, risky design, then the T-72 was the safety-first evolutionary alternative. The T-72 was meant to incorporate the same components as the T-64 except for the engine. By the time it was put into production, only the main weapon fit and ammunition were the same.

PROTECTION

There has been considerable progress in the level of protection of the T-72 over the years. Additionally there is a clear distinction between those tanks built for the Warsaw Pact, and those offered for sale to client states and political allies. The latter lacked the latest laminate armour available to the manufacturers, and the internal, radiation-resistant, liners that shield the crew compartment.

Early T-72s have welded steel turrets and hulls with the frontal arc of the hulls covered in laminated, passive armour. Later T-72s had more advanced armoured packages. The T-72B for example has appliqué, passive armour bulges to its turret sides, and reactive armour bricks fitted to its hull and turret top.

FIREPOWER

The main gun of the T-72 is the same as that of the T-64, a 125mm smoothbore cannon. A revised, although still temperamental, autoloader is fitted, as is a modified ammunition carousel containing 22 rounds. It is thought that the carousel is awkward to reload. Unlike that of the T-64, the T-72's anti-aircraft machine gun cannot be fired from under armour.

Fire control is fairly basic, although a laser rangefinder is integral with the gunner's sight. From the T-72B onwards, a laser beam-riding missile, the AT-11 Sniper missile is fitted. This can be used against high priority targets up to range of 5,000 metres. Six of these missiles are normally carried along with 39 cannon rounds.

MOBILITY

When compared to the T-64, the T-72 has a sturdier, less complex, torsion bar suspension and a simpler, cheaper engine. On paper the T-72 may be less agile

T-72s on the march.   *(Courtesy of Will Fowler)*

than the T-64, but is more reliable and easier to maintain.

The latest variant of the tank, the T-72BM has a more powerful engine.

ASSESSMENT

The T-72 is less sophisticated than the T-64, but at 40% of the price, a cost-effective alternative. When compared to the best of contemporary Western tanks however, the T-72 looks vulnerable. Sometimes apparent bargains have hidden costs!

Widely distributed on the world market, in many ways the T-72 is the true successor to the ubiquitous T-55. The greatly improved T-72B came into service in 1985. The export version of the T-72B, the T-72S, came into service in 1987. This has less sophisticated armour but a more powerful engine. The latest model, the T-72BM, came into service in 1992. It incorporates the best features of previous variants. Some sixteen states use the tank in all its models. It has been produced under licence in the Soviet Union, Czechoslovakia, Poland, Iraq and Yugoslavia.

SERVICE STATUS

In service with Algeria, 300 tanks. Bulgaria, 333 tanks. Cuba, 75 tanks. CIS, 15,000 tanks of which 1,938 are in service with Russia, many more are in storage. Czech Republic, 542 tanks. Finland, 162 tanks. Hungary, 138 tanks. India, 1,100 tanks. Iran, 200 tanks. Iraq, 200 tanks. Libya, 260 tanks. Poland, 717 tanks. Romania, 30 tanks. Slovakia, 912 tanks. Syria, 1,500 tanks. Ukraine, 1,320 tanks. Yugoslavia (Serbia/Montenegro), 250 tanks.

(T-72S)

Prototype:	1970
In service:	1972 (T-72S in service 1987)
Crew:	3
Armament:	Main, 125mm. Secondary, 1 x 7.62mm MG, anti-aircraft 1 x 12.7mm MG
Combat weight:	44,500kg (the T-72B weighs 46,000kg)
Power-to-weight ratio:	18.9hp/t
Ground pressure:	0.90kg/cm^2
Length gun forward:	9.53m
Hull length:	6.95m
Hull width:	3.59 (including skirts)
Height (to commander's cupola):	2.222m
Ground clearance:	0.49m
Power pack:	V-12 multi fuel (V84) 840hp engine. (Earlier variants of the tank had a less powerful engine generating 740-780hp.)
Max road speed:	60km/h
Max range (internal fuel):	480km.
Fording (unprepared):	1.8m
Gradient:	60%
Side slope:	40%
Vertical obstacle:	0.85m

T-72 MBT in Israeli hands.   *(Copyright of Marsh Gelbart)*

MANUFACTURER: SOVIET MILITARY INDUSTRIES

BACKGROUND

With the T-80, the Soviet Union attempted to rationalise its tank fleet. Rather than having the "advanced" T-64, and the "basic" T-72, the T-80 was intended to meld together the best qualities of both. The T-80 has grown in cost, weight and capability since 1979 when the basic T-80 was introduced, through to the 1990s with the arrival of the latest model the T-80UM.

PROTECTION

The T-80 has in its various models used the latest Soviet and CIS developments in laminated armour and new generation reactive armour. Both offer a degree of protection against HEAT and APDS projectiles. Substantial improvements in survivability began with the introduction of the T-80U in 1985. The multi-layered protection of the latest T-80 incorporates first generation active armour defence suites. Active armour as fitted to late models T-80s is of two kinds. Firstly the Shtora-1 system, this attempts to decoy and jam the guidance systems of incoming missiles through intense infra-red

pulses. Secondly, through a combination of sensors including millimetric radar, the more advanced Arena system automatically detects incoming projectiles, and launches a screen of mini-slugs to disrupt, deflect or destroy them.

Whilst late models of the T-80 have a comprehensive self-protection suite, it is notable that the CIS does not appear to place the same level of trust in ceramic, laminated, armour as do Western manufacturers of modern MBTs.

Like most leading MBTs, the T-80 has NBC protection and automatic fire detection/suppression systems.

FIREPOWER

The T-80 uses the same 125mm weapon as the T-64 and T-72. The tank has a three-man crew and an autoloader is fitted. As with its predecessors, the tank's capacity to fight from a hull down position is impeded by its inability to depress its cannon beyond minus five degrees. Ammunition stowage and the type of autoloader follow the pattern of the T-72. The fire control system of the T-80 has seen incremental improvements. Starting

T-80UD, the diesel powered variant of the T-80.   (Courtesy of the Tank Museum)

with the T-80U from about 1992, T-80s have been fitted with thermal imagers.

The T-80 can fire the AT-11 Sniper laser beam-riding missile from its cannon. Up to six of these 5,000 metre range missiles are carried.

MOBILITY
The most radical design departure for the T-80 was the installation of various powerful gas-turbine engines. The experiment with turbine power has proved to be a mixed achievement. Although these engines give unprecedented agility, their fuel thirsty nature has imposed a considerable logistic burden. Indeed in 1988 the T-80UD, was fitted with a diesel engine that generates 1,100hp.

ASSESSMENT
The T-80 is the successor to the T-64. It replaces the latter's problematical power pack and temperamental running gear. Recent events in Chechnya demonstrate that the tank's protection remains questionable, despite the advent of active armour systems. The Ukraine builds a modified version known as the T-84 – see relevant entry.

SERVICE STATUS
In service with China, numbers unknown. Russia, 3,144 tanks. Ukraine, 345 tanks.

(details for the T-80U, unless indicated otherwise)

Prototype:	Baseline T-80, 1976
In service:	T-80U, 1985
Crew:	3
Armament:	Main, 125mm cannon. Secondary, coaxial 1 x 7.62mm MG, anti-aircraft 1 x 12.7mm MG
Combat weight:	46,000kg. (T-80 43,000kg, T-80BV/ T-80BVK 45,000kg)
Power-to-weight ratio:	27.20hp/t. (T-80 UD 23.91hp/t T-80B 25.90hp/t)
Ground pressure:	0.93kg/cm²
Length gun forward:	9.66m
Hull length:	7.0mm
Hull width:	3.59m
Height (to commander's cupola):	2.2m
Ground clearance:	0.446m
Power pack:	1,250hp turbine with manual transmission. (T-80B 1,000hp with manual transmission. T-80UD 1,100hp diesel)
Max road speed:	70km/h
Max range (internal fuel):	335km
Fording (unprepared):	1.2m. (T-80B 1.8m)
Gradient:	63%
Side slope:	46%
Vertical obstacle:	1m

MANUFACTURER: NIZHNYI TAGIL FOR T-90, T-95 UNKNOWN

BACKGROUND

The T-90 appears to be a comprehensive upgrade of the T-72 incorporating features of the T-80. It is rumoured that Russia is reputedly building a high-risk, advanced technology MBT known as the T-95. Given this, the T-90 may be a low-risk, evolutionary, back up vehicle.

PROTECTION

Information available for the T-90 only. Protection appears to be similar to the T-80, although the reactive armour modules mounted on the sides of the hull appear larger and thinner. The Shtora electro-optical jammer system is also fitted, as is the NBC protection expected on modern tanks.

FIREPOWER

Information available for the T-90 only. The same weapon fit as the T-80, comprising a smoothbore 125mm cannon capable of firing the AT-11 Sniper laser beam-riding missile It is believed that 6 Sniper missiles are carried. An autoloader is standard equipment.

MOBILITY

Information available for the T-90 only. The tank is fitted with a Model V-84 diesel of 840hp. Given a combat weight of 46,500kg, then the tank has a power to weight ratio of 18.06hp/t. Maximum road speed is 60 km/h.

ASSESSMENT

It is difficult to understand the design rationale behind the T-90. In some ways it is sub-standard when compared to the T-80. Certainly the T-90's power to weight ratio is inferior to the earlier tank. The T-90 may be symptomatic of the under-funded confusion that has gripped the CIS arms industry on occasion.

Details of the T-95 are very vague and contradictory. The one common strand is that the T-95, be it a rebuild of the T-80 or a new design, will incorporate a low-profile turret. This could entail the fitting of an external gun mounting, rather than a conventional turret.

SERVICE STATUS

The T-90 is thought to be in service in very small numbers in the CIS. The T-95 is thought to be in development.

SPECIFICATIONS – No specifications available

MANUFACTURER: REUMECH

BACKGROUND

As political constraints denied them access to newer equipment, the South Africans were faced with the need to renovate their old Centurion tanks. The Mk 1A Olifant was the response. The Mk 1A concentrated on upgrading firepower and mobility to a level comparable to that of more modern MBTs. The conversion of Centurions to Olifant Mk 1A began in 1974 and continued to 1981.

PROTECTION

The protection level of the Olifant Mk 1A is that of the Centurion. The provision of a diesel engine to replace the original petrol engine, means that the Olifant is less likely to brew-up if hit in the engine compartment.

FIREPOWER

The original 20 pdr weapon of the elderly Centurion was replaced with the very effective British 105mm L7 cannon. However the breech mechanism of the older weapon was retained. Some 72 rounds are stowed for the main armament. Fire control was fairly simple, being that of the basic Centurion, with the addition of a hand-held laser rangefinder and first generation image intensifiers. The tank also used an infra-red searchlight and headlights.

MOBILITY

Although there had been previous South African efforts to re-engine the Centurion, the first widespread and successful programme was that of the Mk 1A Olifant. A diesel engine and additional fuel tanks gave the vehicle a considerable increase in range.

ASSESSMENT

The Olifant Mk 1A was a credible attempt to upgrade and renovate a basically sound but obsolescent MBT. It more than matched the capabilities of MBTs found in neighbouring states during the 1970s.

SERVICE STATUS

The Olifant has only been in service with South African forces. About 300 Centurions were modified to Olifant Mk 1A standard; many have now been further modified to the more capable Olifant Mk 1B.

Olifant Mk 1A   *(Courtesy of the Manufacturer)*

Prototype:	1973
In service:	1978
Crew:	4
Armament:	Main, 105mm rifled cannon. Secondary, coaxial 1 x 7.62mm MG, anti-aircraft 1 x 7.62mm MG
Combat weight:	53,000kg
Power-to-weight ratio:	14.2hp/t
Ground pressure:	1.01kg/cm^2
Length gun forward:	8.29m
Hull length:	7.823m
Hull width:	3.39m
Height (without A-A MG):	2.94m
Ground clearance:	0.5m
Power pack:	V-12 air cooled diesel of 750hp coupled to a semi-automatic transmission
Max road speed:	45km/h
Max range (internal fuel):	250km
Fording (unprepared):	1.2m
Gradient:	60%
Side slope:	30%
Vertical obstacle:	0.91m

MANUFACTURER: REUMECH

BACKGROUND

The Olifant Mk 1B is an extensive rework of the Mk 1A. The upgrade, conducted in the 1980s, used newly developed technologies to improve the fighting qualities of the tank. The Olifant Mk 1B is barely recognisable as once having been a standard Centurion. Considerable improvements in protection and mobility are introduced by the Mk 1B, as are ergonomic changes to decrease the workload on the crew.

PROTECTION

Additional passive armour has been applied to the tanks glacis plate and nose. Stand-off armour is fitted to the turret front, roof and sides. As well as this appliqué armour, a double floor has been added to the tank's belly, this gives increased protection against mines. New side-skirts have also been fitted; these help protect the running gear against attack by HEAT projectiles.

Further measures to improve survivability include, the fitting of a fire detection/suppression system, and the ability to lay a smoke screen by injecting fuel in the engine exhaust.

FIREPOWER

The Mk 1B carries the same 105mm rifled cannon as its predecessor, although the weapon is now fitted with a thermal sleeve. Marginally less ammunition is carried, 68 main rounds as compared to 72. The fire control system has been modernised, both gunner and driver have day/night sights and a laser rangefinder is incorporated in the gunner's sights.

MOBILITY

Substantial changes to the running gear have led to an improved cross-country performance. The Horstmann suspension has been replaced with torsion bar running gear, and hydraulic dampers for the first and last pair of wheel stations have been added. These measures have allowed a much greater range of travel for the road wheels – it has increased from 160mm to 320mm. A more powerful diesel engine has been installed linked to an automatic transmission.

With all these changes, the Olifant Mk 1B has a better power to weight ratio and is faster than the Mk 1A, despite an increase in weight.

Studio shot of the Olifant Mk 1B *(Courtesy of the Manufacturer)*

ASSESSMENT

The Olifant Mk 1B is an impressive upgrade of the basic Centurion, perhaps the most comprehensive and effective renovation of the Centurion ever put into service.

SERVICE STATUS

Only in service with South African forces. It is likely that all Olifants are likely to be upgraded to the Mk 1B standard.

Olifant Mk 1B in the field   *(Courtesy of the Manufacturer)*

Prototype:	1985
In service:	1991
Crew:	4
Armament:	Main, 105mm rifled cannon. Secondary, coaxial 1 x 7.62mm MG, anti-aircraft 1 x 7.62mm MG
Combat weight:	58,000kg
Power-to-weight ratio:	15.5hp/t
Ground pressure:	1.07kg/cm^2
Length gun forward:	10.2m
Hull length:	8.61m
Hull width:	3.42m
Height (to turret top):	3.55m
Ground clearance:	0.345m
Power pack:	V-12 air cooled turbocharged diesel engine of 900hp coupled to an automatic transmission
Max road speed:	58km/h
Max range (internal fuel):	350km
Fording (unprepared):	1.5m
Gradient:	60%
Side slope:	30%
Vertical obstacle:	1.0m

MANUFACTURER: REUMECH

BACKGROUND

The Tank Technology Demonstrator (TTD), is a showcase on tracks. It illustrates the considerable sophistication and skill of South African tank manufacturers, and their ability to integrate advanced technology with operational experience from the bush wars in Angola and Namibia. From the onset of the design project in 1983, the TTD was intended to outmatch any likely MBT acquired by hostile neighbours. Despite its level of sophistication, the TTD is built to be reliable and easy to maintain, even in the harsh conditions of the African bush.

Political changes in South Africa have reduced pressure to build the TTD. However the vehicle is available for production, and many of its advanced components could be applied to other MBTs.

PROTECTION

The front arc of the tank is designed to withstand impact from 125mm smooth bore cannon rounds – as carried by Russian built tanks. Protection is given by multi-spaced armour components, which are likely to incorporate laminated armour. It seems that the TTD has been designed to use alternative armour modules (including reactive armour packs), to meet different expected threat levels. An anti-spall liner is fitted as standard. The sides, rear and turret are designed to withstand the impact of medium calibre rounds, and heavy calibre, artillery air bursts. Ammunition is stowed in the turret bustle; a bulkhead separates the bustle from the crew. Explosion blow-out panels are fitted to help minimise collateral damage, should the bustle be penetrated. Special attention has also been given to surviving mine blasts. There is a degree of built in redundancy for electrical systems, should battle damage be incurred.

The tank has an NBC system, smoke grenades and the ability to lay a smoke screen using its engine. A fire detection/suppression system is fitted to aid crew survival.

TTD at speed in desert terrain.   *(Courtesy of the Manufacturer)*

TTD approaching camera at speed.   *(Courtesy of the Manufacturer)*

Interior of the TTD.   *(Courtesy of the Manufacturer)*

Stationary TTD from the side.   *(Courtesy of the Manufacturer)*

FIREPOWER

The tank carries a 105mm rifled cannon, fitted with a thermal shroud and muzzle reference system. The weapon is fully stabilised. The turret is designed so that it would be relatively easy to fit a 120mm (or even a 140mm), smooth bore weapon.

The tank has a carousel magazine, mounted in its turret bustle, which holds 16 of the 54 rounds that are stowed aboard the TTD. The magazine feeds rounds automatically to the loader, lightening his work load.

A modern stabilised integrated fire control system is installed. Both commander and gunner have monitors for a thermal camera, the commander has third-generation image intensification sights, and the gunner has laser range finding incorporated in his sights. The fire control system can work in hunter/killer mode. The commander can engage a target himself or hand it over to his gunner. The TTD has a good chance of a first shot kill, against moving targets even when itself on the move.

MOBILITY

The tank is powered by a twin-turbo intercooled V-8 engine of 1,230hp, which offers a very useful power-to-weight ratio. A torsion bar suspension is fitted with hydraulic bump stops and dampers. The seven road wheels have a considerable range of vertical movement – 500mm – to help give a comfortable ride over rough terrain.

ASSESSMENT

The South Africans have designed an excellent fighting machine designed to be easily modernised and kept at the forefront of MBT design. Despite its sophistication the TTD is rugged. The only problem with the TTD is that it is unlikely to be produced in the near future, unless further funding is made available.

SERVICE STATUS

Not in service. Development stage only.

Prototype:	Not available
In service:	Not in service
Crew:	4
Armament:	Main, 105mm rifled cannon. Secondary, 1 x 7.62mm MG, anti-aircraft 1 x 7.62mm MG
Combat weight:	58,300kg
Power-to-weight ratio:	21.2hp/t
Ground pressure:	0.93kg/cm^2
Length gun forward:	9.88m
Hull length:	7.78m
Hull width:	3.62m
Height (to commanders sight):	2.99m
Ground clearance:	0.50m
Power pack:	V-8 twin-turbocharged intercooled diesel of 1,200hp coupled to an automatic transmission
Max road speed:	71km/h
Max range (internal fuel):	300km
Fording (unprepared):	1.5m
Gradient:	60%
Side slope:	30%
Vertical obstacle:	0.9m

Studio shot of TTD. *(Courtesy of the Manufacturer)*

Like the Israelis, the Swedes have not been one of the major players in tank design, but have been amongst the most innovative. The Stridsvagn 103 MBT with its unique turretless configuration, automatic loader, three-man crew, and a hydraulic suspension system used to train the gun on target, was a startlingly radical design. The Strv 103 has been overtaken by advances in fire control technology. Modern MBTs can fire on the move at moving targets with a good chance of success, but the Strv 103 cannot because of its fixed gun. Nonetheless, the Swedes demonstrated a great talent for unorthodox approaches to the design of MBTs. Further experimentation with an even more radical configuration using an external, turretless gun mounting, was recently abandoned. It failed for economic reasons, not lack of inspiration.

MANUFACTURER: BOFORS

BACKGROUND

At the date of its inception in 1958, the Strv 103 (S-tank) was staggeringly advanced in terms of its layout. Even today the turretless, fixed gun, S-tank has many sophisticated features. The fixed gun is elevated or depressed by tilting the tank, using a hydrogas suspension system. The gun is aimed in azimuth by fine movement of the vehicles' tracks. The vehicle had its engine at the front, a three-man crew in a compact fighting compartment and an autoloader.

The S-tank has been built in three versions. The Strv 103A, the initial service model, was replaced with the Strv 103B which had an integral flotation screen and a dozer blade fitted to its glacis plate. The Strv 103 A/B were the main models in service between 1966 and 1986. From 1986, all S-tanks were gradually rebuilt to the improved Strv 103C standard.

PROTECTION

The tank's radical configuration contributes greatly to its, and its crew's, survival. The S-tank has a very low battlefield signature, and few ballistic shot traps. The crew are situated low down and towards the rear of the vehicle. The vehicles front mounted engine and other sub-components help shield the crew compartment. The commander and driver both have controls to drive the tank, and to fire the armament. The third member of the crew, the radio operator, sits facing the rear. He too has driving controls and is able to reverse the tank and get it out of trouble if required. This duplication of job function allows the crew to continue the battle even if one of them is a casualty.

Recently the Strv 103C have been seen with a new side skirt ingeniously incorporating extra fuel cells, this gives increased range as well as providing protection for its running gear. In wartime the S-tank would be fitted with a screen of angled bars that slot in at the front of the glacis plate. These bars act as a form of stand-off armour to detonate HEAT projectiles.

FIREPOWER

The S-tank is fitted with a 105mm cannon based on the British L7. At 62 calibres, the gun is longer than the standard L7 and gives a higher muzzle velocity. The Swedes have purchased advanced APFSDS ammunition from Israel to increase the weapon's effectiveness. The tank carries 50 rounds of ammunition for its main gun; these are stowed at the rear in the autoloader's magazine. The autoloader allows a high rate of fire of up to 15 rounds a minute. Fire control, available to both commander and driver, is effective but basic, laser rangefinding is available, and the Strv 103 C has an improved ballistic computer.

There are a number of major drawbacks with the S-tank which affect its firepower and the tank's fighting qualities. Firstly the fixed gun means a loss of tactical versatility as the whole tank has to point, in order for it to aim and shoot. Secondly it cannot fire effectively on the move. Thirdly in order to point the tank, the engine, suspension, and tracks must all be fully functioning and not suffering from battle damage.

Stridsvagn 103 MBT – the S-Tank   *(Courtesy of the Manufacturer)*

Stridsvagn 103 MBT at speed.   *(Courtesy of Will Fowler)*

MOBILITY

The S-tank has a unique engine set-up coupling a diesel and a gas turbine. The diesel is used for normal functions, but in combat the turbine adds its output to boost power.

The four road wheels have a sophisticated hydrogas suspension system. This not only gives a good ride cross country but is used to train the main armament.

Because of its layout and integral flotation screen, the tank is particularly easy to rig for amphibious crossings. Given Sweden's terrain this is a useful feature.

The Strv 103C uses a 290hp diesel, rather than the original one of 240hp, to compensate for its increase in weight over earlier S-tanks.

ASSESSMENT

The S-tank has many unique design features which add to its fighting qualities – particularly its survivability. However its fixed gun does impose tactical constraints. As better electronics now allow MBTs to fire at moving targets whilst they themselves are on the move, this has made the S-tank's tactical restrictions undesirable.

SERVICE STATUS

Only in service with the Swedish Army. Most of the 300 S-tanks built were converted to Strv 103C standard. Approximately 260 S-tanks remain in use. The number in service is declining as Sweden introduces the Leopard 2.

Prototype:	1961
In service:	Strv 103A 1966. Strv 103C 1986
Crew:	3
Armament:	Main, 105mm rifled cannon. Secondary, coaxial 2 x 7.62mm MG, anti-aircraft 1 x 7.62mm MG
Combat weight:	Strv 103B, 39,700kg. Strv 103C, 42,500kg
Power-to-weight ratio:	Strv 103B, 18.4hp/t. Strv 103 C, 18.35hp/t
Ground pressure:	Strv 103B, 1.04kg/cm². Strv 103C, 1.17kg/cm²
Length gun forward:	8.99m
Hull length:	7.04m
Hull width:	3.63m
Height (to commander's cupola):	2.14m
Ground clearance:	0.4m
Power pack:	Strv 103B, Rolls Royce K60 diesel of 240hp plus a Boeing 533 gas turbine of 490hp used for combat boost. Strv 103C, Detroit Diesel 6V-53T of 290hp plus the same turbine as the Strv 103B. S-tank engines are linked to an automatic transmission
Max road speed:	50km/h (When amphibious, the tank can travel at 6km/h)
Max range (internal fuel):	400km
Fording (unprepared):	1.5m
Gradient:	60%
Side slope:	40%
Vertical obstacle:	0.9m

MANUFACTURER: SWISS FEDERAL ARMAMENT
WORKS

BACKGROUND
The Pz 61 was Switzerland's first indigenous tank design.
It had a long gestation period. Whilst the project dated
back to 1951, the first prototype was not built until 1958.
Pre-production models experimented with a succession
of weapons, before standardising on the excellent British
105mm rifled cannon. Because of its long development
process, the Pz 61 did not start entering into service
until 1965.

PROTECTION
The tank has a cast hull and turret; the latter lacks a
bustle. The turret's egg shaped profile, which assists
ballistic protection, is reminiscent of the Soviet T-54/55
series of MBTs. The Pz 61 has slightly greater
dimensions than the T-54/55. Its thickness of armour is
somewhat less, despite a comparable weight. An NBC
system is fitted as standard.

FIREPOWER
A slightly modified, British designed, 105mm rifled
cannon is carried. The coaxial weapon was initially a
20mm cannon, replaced on later models with a 7.5mm
machine gun. Optics and fire control are average for a
tank of the Pz 61's vintage. The main cannon is not
stabilised. Strangely the loader's cupola is higher than
that of the commander's and blocks some of his field of
view.

MOBILITY
A relatively low battle weight coupled to a 630hp engine,
gives a better power to weight ratio than many of the
tank's contemporaries. The tank is narrower than the
norm for a vehicle of its weight, which gives the Pz 61
an advantage when manoeuvring in tight corners. The
track is all steel, and the suspension system employs
Belleville washers on each of the independently mounted
road wheels.

ASSESSMENT
The tank vindicated Switzerland's efforts in
manufacturing its own design. However the Pz 61 is very
much a machine of the late 1950s. The vehicle is being
withdrawn from service.

Posed shot of an early PZ 61 with a 20 mm cannon as a secondary armament.   *(Courtesy of the Manufacturer)*

SERVICE STATUS

Only in service with Switzerland. Of 150 ordered, 117 are still in use but that figure is declining.

Later Pz 61 with the coaxial cannon replaced with a 7.5 mm machine gun. *(Courtesy of the Manufacturer)*

Prototype:	1958
In service:	1965
Crew:	4
Armament:	Main, 105mm rifled cannon. Secondary, coaxial 1 x 7.5mm MG, anti-aircraft 1 x 7.5mm MG
Combat weight:	38,000kg
Power-to-weight ratio:	17hp/t
Ground pressure:	0.85kg/cm^2
Length gun forward:	9.43m
Hull length:	8.28m
Hull width:	3.08m
Height (to commander's cupola):	2.72m
Ground clearance:	0.42m
Power pack:	MTU MB 837 Ba-500 V-8 diesel of 630hp coupled to a semi-automatic transmission
Max road speed:	55km/h
Max range (internal fuel):	300km
Fording (unprepared):	1.1m
Gradient:	60%
Side slope:	40%
Vertical obstacle:	0.75m

MANUFACTURER: SWISS FEDERAL ARMAMENT
WORKS

BACKGROUND

An evolutionary development of the Pz 61, the Pz 68
entered into service in 1971. Four variants of the Pz 68
(Mk 1 through to Mk 4) were produced between 1971
and 1984, although differences between them were
marginal. The slightly larger turret from the Pz Mk 3
onwards, was perhaps the most significant change. A
major upgrade programme – the Pz 68/88 project – was
announced in 1988 and carried out through the mid
1990s. All serviceable Pz 68 Mk 3 and Mk 4 tanks were
renovated to this standard, as were 25 of the Mk 2
variant.

PROTECTION

Protection offered by the cast hull and well-shaped turret
is of the same standard as the Pz 61. As well as smoke
grenade launchers, the Pz 68 is fitted with Bofors Lyran
illuminating rockets. The Pz 68/88 has an improved
collective NBC system.

FIREPOWER

The major changes between the Pz 61 and its
successors are in the realms of fire control. Unlike its
predecessor, the Pz 68 has its 105mm cannon fully
stabilised. The Pz 68/88 has a digital ballistic computer,
stabilised gunners' sights, an integrated laser
rangefinder, and a muzzle reference system. All of these
measures improve gunnery accuracy. A modified 120mm
cannon has been trialled in a Pz 68 fitted with appliqué
armour. Status of this project is unknown.

MOBILITY

The Pz 68 was fitted with an up-rated diesel, improved
transmission and revised running gear. Despite a weight
gain of 1,700kg, the Pz 68 only shows a minor drop in
its power to weight ratio when compared to the Pz 61.
Wider tracks incorporating replaceable rubber pads, plus
a slightly longer stretch of track in contact with the
ground, mean only a minimal increase in ground
pressure. The Pz 68/88 has hydraulic bump stops fitted.

ASSESSMENT

The Pz 68 and its subsequent comprehensive upgrade

Pz 68/88 close up.   *(Courtesy of the Manufacturer)*

to the Pz 68/88 are determined attempts to keep an obsolescent tank design current. The Swiss have done a fine job, however the vehicle has probably reached the practical limits for upgrading. The best Swiss tank in service is not the Pz 68/88, but the Leopard 2 which is assembled locally under licence.

SERVICE STATUS
Only in service with Switzerland. 186 Pz 68s are in service and 186 Pz 68/88s.

Prototype:	1968
In service:	1971
Crew:	4
Armament:	Main, 105mm rifled cannon. Secondary, coaxial 1 x 7.5mm MG, anti-aircraft 1 x 7.5mm MG
Combat weight:	39,700kg
Power-to-weight ratio:	16.62hp/t
Ground pressure:	0.86kg/cm²
Length gun forward:	9.49m
Hull length:	6.88m
Hull width:	3.14m
Height (to commander's cupola):	2.75m
Ground clearance:	0.41m
Power pack:	MTU MB 837 Ba-500 V-8 liquid cooled diesel of 660hp coupled to a semi-automatic transmission
Max road speed:	55km/h
Max range (internal fuel):	350km
Fording (unprepared):	1.1m
Gradient:	60%
Side slope:	40%
Vertical obstacle:	0.75m

Pz 68 MBT front left view. *(Courtesy of the Manufacturer)*

Pz 68 MBT front right view. *(Courtesy of the Manufacturer)*

Pz 68/88 MBT front left view. *(Courtesy of the Manufacturer)*

MANUFACTURER: KHARKOV DESIGN BUREAU, MALYSHEV FACTORY

BACKGROUND

The T-84 is the first venture by the newly independent Ukrainian arms industry to enter into the competitive MBT market. The T-84 is closely based on the ex Soviet T-80UD – a diesel powered variant of the T-80 tank – but with some significant improvements.

PROTECTION

The armour suite of the T-84 is basically that of its Soviet predecessor but with some notable additions. The turret of the T-84 is larger than that of the T-80 and is of welded construction. The Ukrainians claim that it has better protection than the single piece cast turret of the T-80UD. It certainly gives more room for the crew and equipment. The tank and turret incorporate second generation reactive armour.

The T-84 has special measures fitted to minimise the radar and thermal signatures. These involve rubber sheeting around prominent angular portions of the tank, plus thermal cladding around the engine compartment. The Shtora-1 electro-optical active protection suite is fitted – as on late model T-80s – and is linked to an instant smoke screen system to help shield the tank.

To further enhance survivability, NBC protection is fitted, as is a fire detection/suppression system.

FIREPOWER

The tank carries the same smooth bore 125mm cannon as its Russian rivals. The Ukrainians state that they have altered the guns mounting to make it easier to change its barrel. The cannon is able to fire the same laser beam-riding missiles as the T-80 MBT. The autoloader appears to be based on that of the T-64. It is claimed that the tank can fire 7 to 9 rounds a minute. Fire control is that of the T-80U, including the option of thermal imaging capability.

MOBILITY

The tank is fitted with a powerful, yet compact, diesel engine of 1,200hp. This is less fuel thirsty than a turbine and is claimed to be more reliable. More powerful diesel engines of up to 1,500hp may soon be available as an optional fit. Suspension is torsion bar.

ASSESSMENT

The T-84 is a serious challenger for sales in the ex-Soviet Unions allies and client states. The tank's diesel engine is likely to appeal to several potential customers. Protection is probably marginally better than on the Russian T-80. The tank, however, still suffers from an

T-84 front left view.   *(Courtesy of Ukrainian Defence Attaché)*

inability to depress its main armament far enough to benefit fully when fighting from hull-down positions.

SERVICE STATUS
Entering into service with the Ukrainian armed forces.

Prototype:	1993
In service:	1995
Crew:	3
Armament:	Main, 125mm smoothbore cannon. Secondary, coaxial 1 x 7.62mm MG, anti-aircraft 1 x 12.7mm MG
Combat weight:	46,000kg
Power-to-weight ratio:	21.7hp/t
Ground pressure:	0.93kg/cm^2
Length gun forward:	9.66m
Hull length:	7.7m
Hull width:	3.77m
Height (to turret roof):	2.215m
Ground clearance:	0.515m
Power pack:	6TD-2 diesel engine of 1,200hp
Max road speed:	60km/h
Max range (internal fuel):	560km
Fording (unprepared):	1.8m
Gradient:	63%
Side slope:	40%
Vertical obstacle:	1.0m

Traumatised by wartime experience of too often being out-gunned, and of fielding tanks with inadequate armour, post war British tank design placed a heavy emphasis on protection and firepower. British tanks from Centurion onwards have been well protected. Thanks to the development of Chobham armour, they remain some of the most heavily protected MBTs in use. The price, of course, has been paid in excessive weight and moderate mobility. Chieftain and Challenger 1 had only an average power to weight ratio, and were plagued with some reliability problems with their power pack. Only with the arrival of Challenger 2 has this problem been solved.

Firepower levels of British tanks have also been amongst the highest available. The excellent 105mm rifled cannon was adopted by many tank manufacturers, whilst the 120mm rifled cannon in use on Challenger 2 is an impressive weapon. Fire control on the Centurion was simple and effective, on Chieftain and Challenger 1 too complex and slow. Challenger 2 has seen the introduction of an advanced fire control system, easy to use and which gives a very high probability of a swift kill.

MANUFACTURER: ROYAL ORDNANCE/VICKERS

BACKGROUND

Designed as a heavy cruiser tank at the end of World War II, with protection and firepower as its priority, the Centurion proved to be one of the most successful tanks ever built. The tank underwent substantial upgrading throughout its service. South African and Israeli modifications are so extensive that their Centurions have their own separate entries.

PROTECTION

The Centurion was originally intended to be proof against the German 88mm gun, but over the years it was given substantially improved protection. The Centurion has an all-welded hull and a cast turret. It was the first British tank to incorporate improved ballistic protection by having a sloped glacis. The prototype had a weight of 46,700kg, the Mk 13 a weight of 51,800kg; much of the increase in weight was due to appliqué armour welded or bolted to the hull and turret.

FIREPOWER

The Centurion was originally designed to carry a 17-pounder gun; this was rapidly replaced in service with the 20-pounder. From the Centurion Mk 5/2 of 1959 onwards, the tank was armed with the excellent 105mm rifled cannon. This weapon outclassed the 100mm cannon of the T-55 and compared favourably with the 115mm of the T-62. The 105mm cannon was retro-fitted to older marks of the tank. The 105mm Centurion firing APDS, HESH or HEAT rounds, proved capable of out-fighting more modern tanks. Its continuing effectiveness was demonstrated in the Arab/Israeli wars of 1967, 1973 and 1982.

The original gun control system of the Centurion was simple, rugged and effective. It relied on ranging shots fired from the coaxial machine gun. From the late 1970s, operators of the Centurion gradually replaced this set-up with a variety of targeting lasers and fire control computers, offering greater sophistication and accuracy.

MOBILITY

The Achilles heel of the Centurion was its mobility, despite its effective Horstmann suspension. Powered by a fuel hungry petrol engine, the tank had limited range. Petrol also has a higher fire and explosion risk than diesel. The Centurion Mk 3 had a fuel capacity of 545

Centurion MBT equipped with weapon simulators for training purposes.   *(Courtesy of Will Fowler)*

litres, and its off-road range was only 50km. Only with the arrival of the Mk 7 in 1954 was fuel capacity substantially increased – to 977 litres – by lengthening the hull.

Those armies that kept Centurions in frontline service longer than the UK – where it was replaced by the Chieftain in the 1960s – made considerable efforts to improve mobility. Jordan and Sweden for instance both replaced the original petrol engine with more powerful, safer and less fuel demanding diesel power packs. Automatic transmission and hydropneumatic suspension have also been fitted to Jordanian and Swedish Centurions.

ASSESSMENT

A total of 4,423 Centurions were built; construction ended in 1962. Now obsolete, the tank is being phased out of service. The Centurion was a rugged tank, easy to renovate and keep current. Its good basic design, which emphasised protection and firepower, made it effective on the battlefield. Its only shortcoming was its poor mobility, though this was largely alleviated through upgrading.

SERVICE STATUS

Denmark has 128 Centurions, some in storage. Jordan, 293 tanks, the upgraded tank being known as the Tariq. Singapore, 60 tanks. Sweden, 288 tanks. Other main users are Israel, approximately 1,100 in service – see entry for the Sho't, and South Africa, approximately 250 in service – see entry for the Olifant.

(Data for Mk 5 unless indicated otherwise)

Prototype:	1944
In service:	Mk 1 1946. (Mk 5 in service 1956, Mk 13 1962.)
Crew:	4
Armament:	Main, 1 x 83.4mm rifled cannon (Up-gunned Centurions from Mk 5/2 onwards 1 x 105mm rifled cannon) Secondary, coaxial 7.62mm MG, anti-aircraft 1 x 7.62mm MG (Some 105mm armed Centurions carried a 12.7mm MG gun for ranging purposes)
Combat weight:	50,728kg (Mk 13 – 51,820kg)
Power-to-weight ratio:	12.81hp/t (Mk 13 – 12.54hp/t)
Max speed:	34.6km/h
Ground pressure:	0.9kg/cm^2 (Mk 13 – 0.95kg/cm^2)
Length gun forward:	9.83m (Mk 13 – 9.854m)
Hull length:	7.556m (MK 13 – 7.823m)
Hull width:	3.39m
Height (to commander's cupola):	2.94m (Mk 13 – 3.01m)
Ground clearance:	0.46m (Mk 13 – 0.51m)
Power pack:	Rolls Royce Mk IVB V-12 liquid cooled petrol engine of 650hp, coupled to a Merrit-Brown manual transmission
Max road speed:	35km/h
Max range (internal fuel):	On the road 102km (Mk 13 – 190km)
Fording (unprepared):	1.45m
Gradient:	60%
Side slope:	30%
Vertical obstacle:	0.91m

MANUFACTURER: VICKERS DEFENCE SYSTEMS

BACKGROUND

The Centurion's replacement, Chieftain was based on the design philosophy of its predecessor, but lacked its commercial success. It introduced some noteworthy features such as the formidable 120mm rifled cannon, and a semi-supine driver's position. What should have been a superb tank was hampered by mechanical unreliability, at least in its early variants.

The tank was produced in several models. The Mk 3 and the Mk 5 were the major new-build production versions for British use. They were later significantly modernised up to MK 11 and Mk 12 standards. The most notable versions built for export, were the Shir 1 and Shir 2 for Iran. The former was also adopted by Jordan whilst the latter, although never delivered to Iran, was the progenitor of the Challenger 1.

PROTECTION

The Chieftain has a hull and turret of cast and rolled steel welded together. The tank has an excellent ballistic shape which increased its chances of survival on the battlefield. Like the Centurion the Chieftain wears side-skirts to minimise damage to its running gear from HEAT projectiles. The supine position of the driver helped to keep hull height down.

Late model rebuilds of the Chieftains, the Mks 11 and 12, are fitted with Stillbrew armour. This appliqué, composite armour gives increased protection against both HEAT and kinetic energy projectiles.

FIREPOWER

The Chieftain is armed with the L11A5 120mm rifled cannon covered in a thermal shroud. This gun is superior to weapons carried by the Chieftains contemporaries. The early Chieftains suffered from an over complex fire control system. The late model rebuilds, the Mk 11 and 12, are fitted with a fully integrated fire control system including thermal imaging capabilities. This enhances gunnery accuracy.

Chieftain from the front   *(Courtesy of John Norris)*

Chieftain on the move.   *(Courtesy of John Norris)*

Chieftain MBT showing its 120 mm rifled cannon to good effect.   *(Courtesy of Will Fowler)*

Pair of British Chieftains on exercise.

(Courtesy of John Norris)

MOBILITY

The basic problem with Chieftain's mobility came about because its weight became too much for its automotive power. A growth in weight throughout its development, put a strain on its power pack, transmission and running gear. The developers had hoped for a battle mass of 45,000kg. The prototype tank weighed 49,500kg, the first production 53,800kg and the Mk 5 55,000kg excluding appliqué armour! The engine fitted was to suffer a reputation for unreliability because of this. From the Mk 2, the first Chieftain to see service, to the Mk 5, the last major new-built variant, engine power was increased from 650hp to 720hp.

ASSESSMENT

The Chieftain was a formidable tank for its time, despite below average mobility. It offered superior protection and firepower when compared to its contemporaries. It would have enjoyed considerably more commercial success if political considerations had not stopped its export to the Israelis and further deliveries to Iran.

SERVICE STATUS

Iran, 250 tanks but serviceability is doubtful. Jordan, 90 to 100 Chieftains captured by Iraq from Iran and handed over – their service status is unknown. Kuwait, approximately 20 remain in service. Oman 24 tanks. United Kingdom, 60 tanks, plus 412 in store.

(Data for the Mk 5 unless indicated otherwise)

Prototype:	1959
In service:	1963
Crew:	4
Armament:	Main, 120mm rifled cannon. Secondary, coaxial 1 x 7.62mm MG, anti-aircraft 1 x 7.62mm MG. Those Chieftains not fitted with a fully integrated fire control system carried a 12.7mm MG for ranging purposes
Combat weight:	Mk 3, 54,100kg. Mk 5, 55,000kg
Power-to-weight ratio:	Mk 3, 13.31hp/t. Mk 5, 13.63hp/t
Ground pressure:	Mk 3, 0.84kg/cm^2. Mk 5, 0.91kg/cm^2
Length gun forward:	10.8m
Hull length:	7.52m
Hull width:	3.5m
Height (to commander's cupola):	2.895m
Ground clearance:	0.51m
Power pack:	Mk 3 – Leyland L60 diesel of 720hp coupled to a semi-automatic transmission. The Mk 5 has the same power pack but the engine is up-rated to 750hp
Max road speed:	48km/h
Max range (internal fuel):	500km
Fording (unprepared):	1.07m
Gradient:	60%
Side slope:	40%
Vertical obstacle:	0.91m

MANUFACTURER: VICKERS DEFENCE SYSTEMS

BACKGROUND

The larger and more sophisticated a tank, the greater the expense. The Vickers Defence system MBT was an attempt to break this ascending spiral of size, complexity and cost. It was aimed at purchasers who demanded a relatively unsophisticated tank, one with a low battle mass, but which had good fighting qualities. In a tank intended to weigh a mere 37,000 kgs, the vehicle incorporated features of the Centurion with aspects of the Chieftain.

PROTECTION

The Vickers Mk 1 was constructed of an all-welded rolled steel hull and an all-welded turret. The tank lacked the weight of armour associated with its heavier contemporaries. The Centurion's maximum concentration of armour was on its turret front at approximately 150mm, that of the Vickers Mk 1 was 80mm in the same position. Whilst the ballistic shape of the Vickers Mk 1 was superior to the Centurion, its basic survivability was not as good.

FIREPOWER

The Tank carried the excellent L7 105mm rifled canon. A lot of firepower for a small fighting vehicle. Components of the Centurion's fire control system were incorporated, such as a 12.7mm ranging machine gun.

MOBILITY

The tank was fitted with a Leyland diesel of 650hp, a modified version of that powering the Chieftain and a similar transmission. This gave a slightly disappointing power to weight ratio. The torsion bar suspension system was given a smoother ride with hydraulic shock absorbers for three road wheels on each side.

ASSESSMENT

The tank met its set design criteria. It was more than adequate to meet the needs of those countries in Africa and Asia at which it was aimed.

SERVICE STATUS

The tank did not sell as well as it deserved. It saw service in Kuwait – 70 tanks, mostly lost during the Iraqi invasion. The Mk 1 in a modified form, the Vijayanta, was produced for India in large numbers (see relevant entry).

Prototype:	1963
In service:	1965 – Indian Vijayanta, 1970, Kuwaiti Mk 1
Crew:	4
Armament:	Main, 105mm rifled cannon. Secondary, coaxial 1 x 7.62mm MG, ranging 1 x 12.7mm MG
Combat weight:	38,600kg
Power-to-weight ratio:	16.83hp/t
Ground pressure:	0.87kg/cm^2
Length gun forward:	9.73m
Hull length:	7.92m
Hull width:	3.17m
Height (to turret roof):	2.44m
Ground clearance:	0.41m
Power pack:	Leyland L60 Mk 4B liquid cooled diesel of 650hp coupled to a semi-automatic transmission
Max road speed:	48km/h
Max range (internal fuel):	480km
Fording (unprepared):	1.14m
Gradient:	60%
Side slope:	30%
Vertical obstacle:	0.9m

Vickers MBT, original variant.   *(Courtesy of the Tank Museum)*

MANUFACTURER: VICKERS DEFENCE SYSTEMS

BACKGROUND
A marked improvement on its predecessor, the Vickers Mk 3 was aimed at a similar market – discerning customers in developing countries. The tank was given a new turret and a more powerful engine. It was built from 1978 onwards, production still available as required.

PROTECTION
The Mk 3 benefits from an improved turret with a cast front and a more rounded profile, this offers greater ballistic protection than that of the Mk 1. Otherwise the level of protection is the same.

FIREPOWER
A modern fire control system is installed. This incorporates day/night sights and a laser range finder, thus increasing speed and accuracy of gun laying. An upgraded gun stabilisation system is also provided.

The tank retains the L7 105mm cannon, now fitted with a thermal sleeve, and the 12.7mm heavy machine gun of the Mk 1. The latter was retained, even though largely redundant as a ranging instrument, because of its utility against soft-skinned and lightly armoured targets. None of the 50 rounds of 105mm ammunition carried, is stored above the turret line.

MOBILITY
The Vickers Mk 3 was provided with a more powerful American diesel this gives the tank a better power to weight ratio, despite its increased weight. The running gear remained unchanged.

ASSESSMENT
The Mk 3 was an evolutionary improvement on the MK 1. Protection and mobility were augmented. Encouraged by interest in the Mk 3, Vickers developed the Mk 3 (I) in 1986 a much more streamlined and impressive looking fighting vehicle. This variant never went into production – a pity as its 850hp Perkins diesel, wider tracks, improved running gear and suspension gave the vehicle greatly increased mobility. An advanced Marconi fire control system plus a muzzle reference system would have increased gun accuracy.

SERVICE STATUS
The Mk 3 was purchased by Kenya – 76 in service, and by Nigeria where at least 108 are in service. It has been suggested that Nigeria bought a substantial number of Mk 3s to increase their inventory in 1991.

Vickers Main Battle Tank MK3.   *(Courtesy of the Manufacturer)*

Prototype:	1975
In service:	1978
Crew:	4
Armament:	Main, 105mm rifled cannon. Secondary, coaxial 1 x 7.62mm MG, ranging 1 x 12.7mm MG, anti-aircraft 1 x 7.62mm MG
Combat weight:	40,000kg
Power-to-weight ratio:	18hp/t
Ground pressure:	0.89kg/cm^2
Length gun forward:	9.788m
Hull length:	7.92m
Hull width:	3.17m
Height (to turret roof):	2.47m
Ground clearance:	0.43m
Power pack:	Detroit Diesel 12V-71T air-cooled, turbocharged diesel of 725hp coupled to semi-automatic transmission
Max road speed:	50km/h
Max range (internal fuel):	530km
Fording (unprepared):	1.1m
Gradient:	60%
Side slope:	30%
Vertical obstacle:	0.8m

Vickers Main Battle Tank Mk 3.

(Courtesy of Will Fowler)

MANUFACTURER: VICKERS DEFENCE SYSTEMS

BACKGROUND

The Khalid owes its origins to an Iranian request in 1974, for an improved Chieftain. This vehicle, known as the Shir 1, was never to be delivered because of political change in Iran – the order was cancelled in 1979. Jordan ordered 274 of this new improved Chieftain after Iran cancelled its order. With minor modifications to suit Jordanian operational requirements, the new tank – now renamed the Khalid – was delivered to Jordan from 1981.

PROTECTION

The same as the Chieftain, there is the possibility of armour upgrades if the funding is forthcoming. From 1987, a fire detection/suppression system was fitted to the tank.

FIREPOWER

The same weapon fit as Chieftain, a 120mm rifled cannon. The fire control system is very similar to that of late model Chieftains such as the Mk 12. A Barr & Stroud laser rangefinder is incorporated, and the commander has a day/night sight which accepts input from the fire control computer.

MOBILITY

This characteristic shows a dramatic improvement over the baseline Chieftain. The Khalid is equipped with a 1,200hp diesel which gives an impressive power to weight ratio. An automatic transmission is fitted, as is an improved variant of Chieftain's suspension system with a greater range of movement for the wheels. The new suspension allows a better ride over rough terrain.

ASSESSMENT

The Khalid is the tank that the Chieftain should have been. It maintains all the fine points of the Chieftain and adds a powerful, more reliable engine and running gear.

SERVICE STATUS

Some 247 are in service with Jordan.

(The same as the late model Chieftain except for the following)

Combat weight:	58,000kg
Power pack:	Perkins Engines Condor V-12 diesel of 1,200hp, coupled to a automatic transmission
Power-to-weight ratio:	20.68hp/t
Hull length:	8.39m
Hull width:	3.518m
Height:	3.012m

Khalid MBT before delivery to Jordan.

(Courtesy of the Tank Museum)

MANUFACTURER: VICKERS DEFENCE SYSTEMS

BACKGROUND

The Challenger evolved from the Shir 2, itself an improved Chieftain, ordered by Iran but never delivered. The Challenger has many notable improvements when compared to the Chieftain. The pivotal change is in the area of protection. Chobham armour was introduced for the first time on an in-service MBT.

PROTECTION

The introduction of Chobham armour – a form of ceramic and metal laminate – gives the Challenger greatly improved protection against both chemical energy projectiles such as HEAT and kinetic projectiles such as APDS. Chobham provides the yardstick by which other composite armour is measured. Chobham armour gives the Challenger 1 turret a characteristic angular and slab-sided appearance.

During the Gulf War, 200-plus Challengers were sent out to the conflict. Many were given further protection from appliqué armour suites. Reactive armour, designed by Royal Ordnance, was fitted to the tanks glacis and

nose. Passive armour modules built by Vickers, were attached to the side-skirts and hull sides. On the spot modifications also allowed the tank to inject atomised fuel into its exhaust, in the same way as Soviet tanks, to provide an instant smoke screen. No Challenger was knocked out by enemy armour during the Gulf war.

FIREPOWER

The tank carries the L11A5 120mm rifled cannon that equips the Chieftain and Khalid. The fire control and gunnery observation systems are enhanced versions of those fitted to the earlier tanks. The Thermal Observation and Gunnery Sight (TOGS), has been a particularly effective addition. One of the lessons of the Gulf War was that thermal imaging sights are vital in order to maximise firepower capabilities.

Advanced ammunition also played its part in increasing the impact of Challenger on the battlefield. Rounds developed for the Challenger 2's improved L30 gun, were adopted to be fired from the Challenger 1's weapon. These included a new tungsten tipped APFSDS round and a depleted uranium round. It is probable that less than 100 of the latter were fired in anger by

Challenger 1 facing the camera. Tank fitted with weapon simulators for taining purposes.   *(Copyright of Marsh Gelbart)*

Challenger 1 from the front. *(Courtesy of Will Fowler)*

Challenger 1 moves through the mud, the tank is fitted with training simulators for training purposes.

(Copyright of Marsh Gelbart)

Challenger, the tungsten rounds proving more than adequate. Some 300 Iraqi MBTs were destroyed by Challengers. Up to 64 rounds – which have a separate projectile and charge – are carried.

MOBILITY
The Challenger 1 is powered by the same engine as the Khalid. The Challenger 1 still has a respectable power to weight ratio, but is marginally under-powered when compared to the Khalid. The running gear utilises hydropneumatic suspension which allows improved agility over rough terrain.

At the time of the Gulf War, provision was made for the Challenger 1 to be equipped with external/detachable fuel tanks of 200 litres capacity to increase range.

Any shortcomings in the vehicle were to have been addressed by the Challenger 1 Improvement Programme (CHIP). CHIP entails automotive improvements with the potential to increase the tank's manoeuvrability and reliability. At the time of writing, it seems more likely that the UK will purchase further Challenger 2s rather than introduce all aspects of the CHIP programme.

ASSESSMENT
An impressive tank that has proved itself in battle. Its design concentrates on survivability and firepower, but mobility has not been allowed to come a poor third as in earlier post-war British tanks.

SERVICE STATUS
United Kingdom, 426 tanks.

Prototype:	1983
In service:	1984
Crew:	4
Armament:	Main, 120mm rifled cannon. Secondary, coaxial 1 x 7.62mm MG, anti-aircraft 1 x 7.62mm MG
Combat weight:	62,000kg
Power-to-weight ratio:	19.35hp/t
Ground pressure:	0.97kg/cm^2
Length gun forward:	11.56m
Hull length:	8.327m
Hull width:	3.42m
Height (to turret roof):	2.5m
Ground clearance:	0.5m
Power pack:	Perkins Engines Condor 12V 1200 liquid cooled diesel of 1,200hp, coupled to a David Brown Gear Industries automatic transmission
Max road speed:	56km/h
Max range (internal fuel):	450km
Fording (unprepared):	1.1m
Gradient:	60%
Side slope:	40%
Vertical obstacle:	0.9m

MANUFACTURER: VICKERS DEFENCE SYSTEMS

BACKGROUND

The Challenger 2, beat off competition from the American M1A2 Abrams, the French Leclerc and the German Leopard 2 (Improved), to satisfy the British Army's Staff Requirement 4026 of 1987. This Staff Requirement called for a tank to replace the remaining Chieftains still in service. The Challenger 2's hull and engine were closely based on the Challenger 1, but the turret and running gear show substantial improvements over those of the earlier tank.

PROTECTION

The turret of the Challenger 2 incorporates second generation Chobham armour. This offers enhanced protection against both kinetic and chemical energy projectiles. Survivability is further augmented by having all ammunition charges stowed below the level of the turret ring in armoured containers, thus minimising the chance of explosion.

The Challenger 2 also mounts attachments for a dozer blade so that the tank can dig its own shell-scrape for cover.

FIREPOWER

The Challenger 2 is equipped with particularly sophisticated gunnery control. This is based upon the Canadian CDC Mission Management Computer System. This system integrates input from the TOGS thermal imager, the gunner's sight and laser rangefinder and those of the tank commander. This allows the Commander to use his separate sight and monitor to acquire a target. The commander can then automatically lock on and bring the gun to bear, designate the target to the gunner, and then search for additional targets whilst the gunner engages the first. This new system is intended to remedy some flaws in the fire control of the Challenger 1. During the Gulf War it was evident that whilst the TOGS equipped Challenger 1 was able to identify and engage stationary targets at a greater range than the M1A1 Abrams, the Challenger 1's gunnery system was slower to engage moving targets. The Challenger 2 has rectified this problem.

The 120mm rifled cannon is the new 55-calibre L30. This weapon is chrome-lined to increase durability and maximise accuracy. The weapon fires a family of advanced ammunition. These include the CHARM 3 depleted uranium round This along with tungsten

Challenger 2 at rest.   *(Courtesy of John Norris)*

Challenger on the move.   *(Courtesy of Will Fowler)*

Challenger at speed.   *(Courtesy of the Manufacturer)*

APFSDS rounds offer greater penetration against modern reactive and passive armour. Up to 50 rounds are carried.

The coaxial machine gun has been replaced with a 7.62mm chain gun which is more effective against soft targets.

MOBILITY
The tank has a modified version of the engine and transmission of the Challenger 1. These modifications, along with an improved hydropneumatic suspension, aid cross country mobility and manoeuvrability in confined spaces. Range has also been increased by fitting attachment points for external fuel cells. The cells can be jettisoned if the tactical situation calls for it.

A trial vehicle has been run utilising a more powerful German built engine, the MTU 883 V-12 diesel of 1,500hp. To date it seems that the new engine will not be adopted, although it may make the tank more competitive on the export market.

ASSESSMENT
The Challenger 2 along with the Abrams, Leclerc, Leopard 2 (Improved) and Merkava III, is a candidate for the best MBT on the market. The tanks excellent

protection and firepower are to its credit. It is marginally under-powered compared to some of its competitors.

SERVICE STATUS
The UK has ordered 386 of the Challenger 2. Oman has ordered 18.

Prototype:	1990
In service:	1994
Crew:	4
Armament:	Main, 120mm rifled cannon. Secondary, coaxial 1 x 7.62mm Chain Gun, anti-aircraft 1 x 7.62mm MG
Combat weight:	62,500kg
Power-to-weight ratio:	19.2hp/t
Ground pressure:	0.9kg/cm^2
Length gun forward:	11.55m
Hull length:	8.327m
Hull width:	3.52m
Height (to turret roof):	2.49m
Ground clearance:	0.5m
Power pack:	Perkins Engines CV-12 TCA Condor V-12 12-cylinder diesel of 1,200hp coupled to an automatic transmission
Max road speed:	56km/h
Max range (internal fuel):	450km
Fording (unprepared):	1.1m
Gradient:	60%
Side slope:	40%
Vertical obstacle:	0.9m

The US, post war, has produced a series of well-balanced tank designs, with equal weight given to protection, firepower and mobility. Any problems have resulted from a tendency to over engineer the tank. Sometimes sound basic design is of more use than advanced technology.

Protection has been comparable with Soviet tanks with the proviso that as American tanks are bigger, their battle mass tends to be 30% higher than their Russian equivalents.

One initial failing of US tanks was their mediocre firepower. To some extent the US compensated for this by adopting more advanced fire control systems than those used by Eastern bloc tanks. However only when the British L7 105mm rifled cannon was adopted did US tanks reach a satisfactory level of firepower. The 120mm smoothbore cannon carried by the M1 Abrams, is based on a German design.

The US has produced tanks that are mobile with relatively high power to weight ratios. However, only with the appearance of the M60 were petrol engines replaced with diesel power packs and their lower fire risk. The percentage of the internal volume taken up by the tank's power pack, is considerably more than on Soviet designed tanks. Unlike the latter, American tanks have adequate internal fuel storage and do not need to carry potentially hazardous, externally mounted fuel cells.

MANUFACTURER: BUILT IN MANY VARIANTS BY NUMEROUS AUTOMOBILE PLANTS DURING WORLD WAR II

BACKGROUND

Built in enormous quantities in World War II (48,000 plus), the Sherman tank was ubiquitous in the mechanised formations of the Western Allies. Long obsolete the Sherman is still kept in the reserve and training inventories of lesser armies.

PROTECTION

The Sherman was at a disadvantage when compared to its World War II German adversaries. With its high profile, slab-sided design giving it a poor ballistic shape, the Sherman had only fair armour protection.

Those Shermans with petrol engines had a deservedly poor reputation for brewing up when hit.

FIREPOWER

Although the basic Sherman had its rather feeble 75mm gun replaced with the harder hitting 76mm weapon, the only World War II Sherman capable of taking on German armour on even terms was a variant known as the Firefly. The Firefly was equipped with the British 17-pounder gun. The only Sherman equipped with a more powerful, low trajectory weapon, was the Israeli upgrade the M51 Isherman (qv).

MOBILITY

The Sherman was reliable and easily maintained. From 1944, once an earlier suspension was replaced by the new Horizontal Volute Suspension system, the Sherman proved nimble with a good ride.

Many Shermans had fuel hungry petrol engines with a resultant small range in between refuelling.

ASSESSMENT

The Sherman was produced in massive numbers, not because it was a superior weapon of war, but because it was available and could be produced relatively easily. The Sherman Firefly was the only World War II variant with real teeth.

SERVICE STATUS

In reserve service or in storage – in declining numbers – with the following states. Argentina, 96 tanks. Chile, 100 tanks. Paraguay, 5 tanks.

Specifications for M4A3E8 unless indicated otherwise

Prototype:	1941 (Basic Sherman)
In service:	1942 (Basic Sherman). 1943 (Sherman M4A3E8)
Crew:	5
Armament:	Main, 76mm cannon. Secondary, coaxial 7.62mm MG, bow 1 x 7.62mm MG, anti-aircraft 1 x 12.7mm MG
Combat weight:	32,284kg
Power-to-weight ratio:	13.93hp/t
Ground pressure:	0.72kg/cm²
Length gun forward:	7.518m
Hull length:	6.273m
Hull width:	2.667m
Height:	3.425m
Ground clearance:	0.434m
Power pack:	Ford GAA 8-cylinder petrol engine of 450hp coupled to a manual transmission
Max road speed:	48km/h
Max range (internal fuel):	160km/h
Fording (unprepared):	0.914m
Gradient:	60%
Side slope:	30%
Vertical obstacle:	0.609m

World War II M4A3 Sherman. *(Courtesy of the Tank Museum)*

MANUFACTURER: DETROIT TANK PLANT AND AMERICAN LOCOMOTIVE COMPANY

BACKGROUND

The outbreak of the Korean war occurred before a new generation of US tanks had come to fruition. The M47 was a stopgap. The turret of a prototype tank the T42, was mated to the hull of the existing M46 MBT. The resulting tank was produced between 1951 and 1953. Although produced in considerable numbers, the tank was merely an interim measure until the M48 was ready for production.

PROTECTION

Armoured protection for the M47 is inferior to that of the T-54/55 series of Soviet tanks. The M47's turret has a maximum armour thickness of 100mm; the T-55's turret is 203mm thick. Despite its own deficiencies, the T-54/55 is a better protected fighting machine.

FIREPOWER

The M47 carries a 90m cannon, as was intended the gun was a match for the German wartime 88 mm weapon, but in turn is outclassed by the 100mm cannon

carried by the T-54/55.

The tank's stereoscopic sights and analogue ballistic computer were advanced for their time of introduction, but are complex and slow to use.

The M47 had a fifth crewman to operate a hull mounted machine gun. This relic of the Second World War took up valuable space that could have been used to store 90mm cannon rounds. The M47M upgraded variant of 1969 abandoned the fifth crewman.

MOBILITY

The M47 is fitted with a powerful petrol engine, however it is fuel hungry – this restricts the tank's range. In addition petrol engines are more inflammable than diesel ones, when subject to combat damage. The suspension system is torsion bar.

ASSESSMENT

The M47 was the last tank produced by the USA to have such World War Two characteristics as a five-man crew and a hull machine gun. The tank showed signs of its rushed entry into service. It is notable that as soon as the better M48 became available, it supplanted the earlier tank. The M47 became an export item and not a front

M47 in Spanish service.   *(Courtesy of the Tank Museum)*

line tank for US service.

Several companies have introduced update packages to increase all aspects of the M47's fighting qualities. These updates incorporate many design features of the M48 series.

SERVICE STATUS
Greece, has 89 tanks, in store. Iran, less than 150 tanks. South Korea, 400 tanks. Pakistan, 120 tanks. Turkey, 523 tanks.

Prototype:	1950
In service:	1951
Crew:	5
Armament:	Main 90mm rifled cannon. Secondary, coaxial 1 x 7.62mm MG, bow 1 x 7.62mm MG, anti-aircraft 1 x 12.7mm MG
Combat weight:	46,170kg
Power-to-weight ratio:	17.54hp/t
Ground pressure:	0.94kg/cm^2
Length gun forward:	8.51m
Hull length:	6.307m
Hull width:	3.51m
Height (to commander's cupola):	3.02m
Ground clearance:	0.46m
Power pack:	Continental AV1790-5B V-12 air-cooled petrol engine of 810hp coupled to a manual transmission
Max road speed:	48km/h
Max range (internal fuel):	130km
Fording (unprepared):	1.2m
Gradient:	60%
Side slope:	30%
Vertical obstacle:	0.91m

MANUFACTURER: CHRYSLER CORPORATION, FORD MOTOR COMPANY, GENERAL MOTORS, ALCO PRODUCTS

BACKGROUND

The first American tank to discard such World War II features as the bow machine gun. Developed from 1950, the first prototype was built in 1951 and the tank went into service in 1952. The tank went through numerous marks as initial shortcomings in its transmission, engine and running gear were remedied. Up to 11,700 M48s of all marks were built.

The original M48 was replaced in service by the M48A1 which introduced minor changes to the commander's cupola and running gear. The M48A2 introduced a more comprehensive series of changes including, improved fuel supply and efforts to reduce the engines infra-red signature, upgraded gunnery controls and modified running gear. The M48A3, a rebuild of earlier variants, had the most significant changes. These involved the fitting of a diesel engine, and the introduction of other features retrofitted from the M60 tank design. The running gear and fire control system of the M48A3 all benefited. The M48A5, also an exhaustive rebuild of earlier variants, was fitted with a 105mm cannon based on the British weapon, the L7. The new gun greatly increased the fighting ability of the tank.

PROTECTION

The boat shaped hull of the M48 is cast, as is the rather large, and bulky turret. In general the ballistic configuration of hull and turret is good. The tank's main drawback is its height. The original commander's cupola is ludicrously bulky and complex. The M48A5 introduced an Israeli designed, low profile commander's cupola.

The tank has adequate armour protection, but not as thick as some of its adversaries. The maximum armour of its turret, the most likely portion of any tank to be hit, is 110mm. That of the T-55's turret is 203mm. As some shells are stored by the turret ring and in the turret itself, the tank is potentially vulnerable to a catastrophic explosion if the turret is pierced.

Unlike the Centurion and later British tanks, the M48 uses a hydraulic system to traverse the turret rather than an electric motor. The high pressure liquid used in the hydraulic system has been known to cause severe burns to tank crews if it ruptures after battle damage.

FIREPOWER

Early models of the M48 had acceptable firepower in the shape of the M41 90mm gun. Some 54 rounds of cannon ammunition were carried. However when compared to some of its competitors, the tank was under-gunned. Only with the arrival of the M48A5 and its highly effective M68 105mm cannon, has the M48 lived up to its potential.

For its time the tank had an advanced gunnery control system, this involved a coincidence range finder and electromechanical ballistic computer. The sheer complexity of the gunnery system may have daunted all but the best trained crews.

MOBILITY

Early model M48s were fitted with powerful petrol engines. Whilst they give a good power to weight ratio, petrol engines are more fuel hungry than diesels and are more prone to catch fire if hit. With the M48A3 diesel power became standard. Suspension is torsion bar.

ASSESSMENT

Despite a very credible combat record in the hands of the Israelis and others, early variants of the M48 were imperfect products. They were too bulky, carried too small a calibre gun, and until the M48A3 were powered by petrol engines. Only after the appearance of the M48A5 with its 105mm gun, did the M48 become a really dangerous foe on the battlefield.

Many early M48s have been upgraded to a standard equivalent to the M48A5. Germany and Israel carried out particularly extensive upgrades. The German variant – the M48A2GA2 is no longer in service. For information on the Israeli upgrade see the entry for the Magach.

SERVICE STATUS

Several countries maintain early M48 tanks in service or in reserve. Many of the early tanks are being upgraded

M48A1 from side. *(Courtesy of the Manufacturer)*

M48A5 note 105 mm cannon. *(Courtesy of the Manufacturer)*

M48A2 showing a good view of the over complex commander's cupola, also note 105 mm cannon.
(Courtesy of the Manufacturer)

Prototype:	1951 (Baseline M48)
In service:	1952. M48A3, 1967. M48A5, 1975.
Crew:	4
Armament:	Main, 90mm rifled cannon, replaced by 105mm rifled cannon from M48A5 model onwards. Secondary, coaxial 1 x 7.62mm MG, anti-aircraft 1 x 12.7mm MG
Combat weight:	47,173kg, M48A3. 48,987kg, M48A5
Power-to-weight ratio:	17.39hp/t, M48A2. 15.89hp/t, M48A3. 15.31hp/t M48A5.
Ground pressure:	0.83kg/cm^2, M48A3. 0.88kg/cm^2, M48A5
Length gun forward:	8.686m, M48A3. 9.306m, M48A5
Hull length:	6.68m, M48A3. 6.42m, M48A5
Hull width:	3.63m
Height (to turret top):	3.089m M48A2. 3.124m, M48A3. 3.086m, M48A5
Ground clearance:	0.385m, M48A2. 0.486m, M48A3. 0.419m, M48A5
Power pack:	AV-1790-8 Petrol engine of 825hp, M48A2. AVDS-1790-2A Diesel engine of 750hp, M48A2 & M48A5 coupled to an automatic transmission
Max road speed:	48km/h
Max range (internal fuel):	258km, M48A2. 463km, M48A3, 500km M48A5
Fording (unprepared):	1.22m
Gradient:	60%
Side slope:	30%
Vertical obstacle:	0.91m

to at least M48A5 standard. Greece has 988 tanks. Jordan has approximately 200 in its emergency war reserve. Iran, a small number of M48A5s still in service. Israel, about 325 M48A5s in service, most being upgraded to Magach 7 standard. South Korea, 850 M48s all upgraded. Lebanon, 100 tanks. Morocco, 224 tanks. Norway, 38 tanks in store. Pakistan, 280 M48A5s. Portugal, 86 M48A5s. Spain, 164 upgraded M48A5s. Thailand, 150 M48A5s. Taiwan, 100 M48A5 plus 450 upgraded M48H. Turkey, approximately 3,000 upgraded M48s. Although the USA no longer has the M48 in service it is thought that about 500 M48s are kept in storage.

MANUFACTURER: GENERAL DYNAMICS

BACKGROUND

An evolutionary development of the M48 series, the M60 saw the introduction of increased ballistic protection, improved firepower, and increased range and greater safety through the introduction of a diesel engine. A successful venture, over 15,000 M60s have been built.

The first M60 was a hybrid involving a new hull but with the old turret of the M48 fitted with a 105mm cannon. After the baseline M60, the tank went through three distinct marks. The M60A1 had thicker armour, a new turret and improved ammunition stowage. The M60A2, an attempt to fit a new turret with a 152mm gun/missile launcher – it proved to be a technical disaster and is no longer in service. The M60A3 is a product improved M60A1, with substantial improvements to the gun fire control system. Many early M60s are being brought up to M60A3 standards by separate national programmes.

PROTECTION

The tank offers considerably better protection than its predecessor. The hull is cast and welded with an all-cast turret. From the M60A1 onwards, the turret has an improved ballistic shape. It has been suggested that the M60 has a very high, maximum armour thickness on the turret front of 254mm. One problem with the M60 was its ridiculously high and complex commander's cupola. This has been replaced with a simple and more effective, low profile, Israeli designed cupola.

The M60A3 is not only fitted with smoke grenade dischargers, but can generate smoke by injecting a fuel aerosol into its engine exhaust.

The M60A3 is fitted with an improved NBC system and a fire detection/extinguishing system that uses halon gas.

FIREPOWER

The main technological gains in the M60 series are in the realms of firepower. Not only is a 105mm M68 cannon with 63 rounds of ammunition carried as standard, but increasingly sophisticated gunnery controls have been fitted to the M60 series. The M60A1 was equipped with passive night sights as well as a white light/infra-red searchlight. The M60A3 has a sophisticated Hughes fire control system which integrates a laser rangefinder,

M60A1 of US Marine Corps photographed in Jutland on exercise in 1982.   *(Courtesy of the Will Fowler)*

environmental sensors, and a new ballistic computer. From 1980 the fire control system was further improved by the fitting of a Texas Instruments thermal sight which replaced the gunner's passive imaging device. The gun on the M60A3 is stabilised in both elevation and traverse; this capability is being retrofitted to the M60A1.

MOBILITY
The tank has a diesel engine that gives reasonable mobility and a good road range. A torsion bar suspension is standard. Attempts to fit an advanced hydropneumatic suspension were abandoned on the grounds of cost.

ASSESSMENT
The M60 has proved to be an effective fighting vehicle. It has seen combat in several war zones and has acquitted itself well. Although being phased out of US service, the M60 has established itself as a tank that's fairly easy to upgrade. Many M60s still in service, have had their combat performance further enhanced. Companies offering upgrades have installed appliqué armour, 120mm guns, advanced ammunition and more powerful engines. The M60 is likely to be around for many years to come.

SERVICE STATUS
Austria has 169 tanks in service. Bahrain, 106. Egypt, 1700. Greece, 671. Iran, 160. Israel 1,200, most being modernised to Magach standard. Italy, 160 in store. Jordan 218. Oman, 49. Saudi Arabia, 450. Spain, 294. Sudan, 20, probably non-operational. Taiwan, 20. Thailand, 53. Tunisia, 84. Turkey, 1,000 plus. USA, 4297, no longer in frontline service. Yemen, 50, only a small number likely to be operative.

Prototype:	1958
In service:	M60, 1960. M60A1, 1962. M60A3, 1978
Crew:	4
Armament:	Main 1 x 105mm rifled cannon. Secondary 1 x 7.62mm MG, anti-aircraft 1 x 12.7mm MG
Combat weight:	49,714kg, M60. 52,617kg, M60A1/M60A3
Power-to-weight ratio:	15.08hp/t (M60). 14.24hp/t, M60A1/M60A3
Ground pressure:	0.8kg/cm^2, M60. 0.87kg/cm^2, M60A/M60A3
Length gun forward:	9.31, M60. 9.44m, M60A1 & M60A3
Hull length:	6.95m
Hull width:	3.63m
Height (to commander's cupola):	3.21m, M60. 3.27m, M60A1, M60A3
Ground clearance:	0.46m, M60. 0.45m, M60A1/M60A3
Power pack:	Continental AVDS-1790 2A or 2C diesel of 750hp coupled to an automatic transmission
Max road speed:	48.3km/h
Max range (internal fuel):	500km, M60/M60A1. 480km, M60A3
Fording (unprepared):	1.22m
Gradient:	60%
Side slope:	30%
Vertical obstacle:	0.91m

M60A1, again note the enormous and complex commanders cupola. *(Courtesy of the Manufacturer)*

M60A1 initial variant. *(Courtesy of the Manufacturer)*

MANUFACTURER: GENERAL DYNAMICS

BACKGROUND

The M1 grew out of a development project of the early 1970s put out to competitive tender. The winning design was not just an evolutionary improvement over the M60 series, it demonstrated some radical design concepts. Survivability was given much greater emphasis than in previous US designs, perhaps reflecting the lessons of the 1973 Arab/Israeli war. Firepower lethality was increased by improvements in gunnery control and in later models by an increase in gun calibre. The tank's mobility also received attention with some novel solutions.

The M1 Abrams has been built in considerable numbers, close to 9,000 of all variants, although production at present is running at a low level. The basic M1 was built from 1980 through to 1985, when the product Improved M1 replaced it on the production lines with in 1986 until in turn supplanted by the M1A1.

PROTECTION

The original model M1 Abrams was the first American tank to use Britain's Chobham armour. Chobham greatly augments the M1's ability to survive both chemical energy and kinetic energy anti-tank projectiles. The Improved M1 had extra armour over its frontal arc.

All the 105mm ammunition is stored in armoured containers. Most of the ready to use rounds are held in the turret bustle, stowed in specialised compartments. These compartments are intended to vent any explosion upwards through blow out panels if hit and pierced.

The tank has an NBC system and smoke grenade dischargers to complement its survivability.

FIREPOWER

The Abrams in its basic versions carries the US version of the British L7 105 rifled cannon. The cannon is fully stabilised. Depleted uranium rounds were developed for the gun offering greater capability against laminated and spaced armour.

The M1 series are equipped with sophisticated fire control systems including the Hughes thermal imaging camera. Even the base line M1 has a laser range finder, digital fire control computer and stabilised gunner's sights.

Evocative shot of M1 Abrams charging through the sand.   *(Courtesy of the Manufacturer)*

M1A1 Abrams moves along a stream bed.

(Courtesy of the Manufacturer)

A pair of M1 Abrams MBTs.   *(Courtesy of the Manufacturer)*

MOBILITY

The tanks most unusual feature is the use of a gas turbine power pack. The turbine offers more power for its size than a comparable diesel engine. The M1 is a notably fast tank, despite its weight, with impressive acceleration from a standing start. The drawback of a gas turbine when compared to a modern diesel, is that it is more fuel thirsty and imposes an increased logistic burden. This problem is compounded as, unlike other leading tanks, the Abrams does not have an auxiliary power unit (APU). An APU allows a tank to operate its turret and fire control system even when the main engine is not running and the tank is on "silent watch". The M1 – even in its later variants – needs to keep its main engine ticking over. This means further fuel expenditure and a larger thermal and noise signature.

The M1 tank has a torsion bar type suspension. The Improved M1 introduced changes to its suspension to maximise cross country performance.

ASSESSMENT

The M1 and the Improved M1 are radical departures for US tank manufacturers. Protection and survivability show a marked improvement over previous US designs. The turret was designed with upgrading in mind. It proved relatively easy to up-gun to a 120mm weapon in later models of the tank. The only question mark over the M1 remains its thirst for fuel. Unlike the United States, not every army has the lavish logistic capabilities necessary to keep the M1 refuelled and running.

SERVICE STATUS

In service with the US army – 2,374 M1 tanks and 894 Improved M1s are in use. Many of the baseline M1s are to be converted to M1A2 standard.

Prototype:	1976
In service:	1980, M1. 1985, Improved M1.
Crew:	4
Armament:	Main, 105mm rifled cannon, Secondary, coaxial 1 x 7.62mm MG, anti-aircraft, 1 x 12.7mm MG & 1 x 7.62mm MG
Combat weight:	54,545kg, M1. 55,550kg. Improved M1
Power-to-weight ratio:	27.5hp/t, M1. 27hp/t, Improved M1
Ground pressure:	0.96kg/cm²
Length gun forward:	9.77m
Hull length:	7.918m
Hull width:	3.653m
Height (to turret roof):	2.375m
Ground clearance:	0.43m
Power pack:	Textron Lycoming AGT 1500 multi-fuel gas turbine engine of 1,500hp coupled to an automatic transmission
Max road speed:	72.4km/h
Max range (internal fuel):	500km (M1)
Fording (unprepared):	1.22m
Gradient:	60%
Side slope:	40%
Vertical obstacle:	1.24m

MANUFACTURER: GENERAL DYNAMICS

BACKGROUND

From 1985 until 1993, the M1A1 became the main variant of the Abrams in service. Armed with its more powerful 120mm smooth bore cannon and increased armour protection, the M1A1 Abrams is a formidable opponent. From 1992 the M1A1 was supplemented by the more advanced M1A2. The M1A2 uses advances in technology to augment its battlefield effectiveness. The bulk of M1A2s are upgraded older M1s, however a small quantity of brand new M1A2s will continue to be produced in order to preserve US tank production capability.

PROTECTION

Some late model M1A1 tanks have been fitted with depleted uranium armour to supplement the Chobham type passive armour arrays. The heavy inert material – arranged in a type of armour matrix – offers better protection against high density kinetic energy penetrators such as depleted uranium or advanced tungsten long-rod projectiles. These models, the best protected of the M1 Abrams variants, were the spear-point of US armoured formations in Western Germany. They paid a price for their enhanced protection in the form of a reduced power to weight ratio. The M1A1 has an improved NBC system and – along with the smoke grenade launchers long standard on Western tanks – the ability to inject fuel into its engine exhaust to lay down smoke.

The M1A2 has thicker passive armour on its turret roof offering better protection against top attack weapons. However electronics are at the heart of its greater survivability. Environmental sensors, threat detection systems, and an electronic navigation and positioning system are all fitted. This "electronic armour" includes the capacity to transfer electronic data from tank to tank through the Inter-Vehicular Information System (IVIS). The result of all these electronic systems is to enhance tactical awareness and increase chances of survival.

FIREPOWER

From the M1A1, the Abrams main armament was the German 120mm smooth bore cannon, as used by the Leopard 2. Depleted uranium rounds developed for the 120mm weapons were used to good effect in the Gulf War against Iraqi armour.

The M1A2 has superior electronics to heighten the efficiency and speed of gun laying. Perhaps the most significant individual advance is the provision of an independent thermal viewer for the tank commander. Improved situational awareness – an enhanced comprehension of the tactical situation – gives a greater chance of first shot and thus first-kill capability. The ongoing M1A2 System Enhancement Package (SEP), will continue to introduce state of the art electronics to the M1 series.

MOBILITY

From the M1A1 onwards, improved shock absorbers and changes to the suspension have improved the cross-country ride allowing the tank to take full advantage of its powerful engine. Like earlier variants of the Abrams, the M1A1 and M1A2 have excellent acceleration and power to weight ratios. The M1A2 has further upgrades to its suspension and trials have been carried out with a less fuel hungry gas turbine.

M1A2 heading at high speed towards the camera.
(Courtesy of the Manufacturer)

ASSESSMENT

The M1A1 has seen combat in the Gulf War where it proved itself one of the finest MBTs of the 1990s. The tank's thermal imaging camera allowed it to successfully engage Iraqi T-72s, at a range where the Soviet built tank was unable to reply in kind. The M1A1 was also able to withstand impact from 125mm tank rounds, with relative impunity, even at close range.

Whilst the M1A1 demonstrated considerable improvements in protection and firepower, the M1A2 showed an even more innovative approach to increase the Abrams fighting qualities. Through the use of electronics to assist battlefield management, reduce crew workload and amplify situational awareness, the M1A2 is potentially one of the most dangerous opponents that can be met on the battlefield.

Any qualms about the tank relate to the fuel thirsty engine and the initial lack of an APU to allow "silent watch". Second generation gas turbines for the Abrams are being trialled, whilst the installation of APUs into 1,500 M1A1s is continuing apace.

SERVICE STATUS

In service with Egypt, 200 M1A1 tanks, others on order. (The M1A1 is being built under licence in Egypt). Kuwait, 50 M1A2s. Saudi Arabia, 315 M1A2s. US Army and Marines, over 7,719 M1 Abrams tanks of various variants are in service, including 5,000 M1A1s. Various upgrading programmes will eventually bring the bulk of M1s to M1A2 standard.

Prototype:	1981, M1A1. 1990, M1A2
In service:	1985, M1A1. 1992, M1A2
Crew:	4
Armament:	Main, 120mm smoothbore cannon. Secondary, coaxial 1 x 7.62mm MG, anti-aircraft, 1 x 12.7mm MG & 1 x 7.62mm MG
Combat weight:	57,155kg, M1A1. 63,738kg, M1A1 with depleted uranium armour. 61,690kg, M1A2
Power-to-weight ratio:	26.24hp/t, M1A1. 23.53hp/t, M1A1 with depleted uranium armour. 24.31hp/t, M1A2
Ground pressure:	0.96kg/cm^2
Length gun forward:	9.83m all 120mm armed variants
Hull length:	7.918m
Hull width:	3.66m
Height (to turret roof):	2.44m
Ground clearance:	0.432m
Power pack:	Textron Lycoming AGT 1500 multi-fuel gas turbine engine of 1,500hp coupled to an automatic transmission
Max road speed:	66.8km/h, M1A1
Max range (internal fuel):	460km, M1A1
Fording (unprepared):	1.22m
Gradient:	60%
Side slope:	40%
Vertical obstacle:	1.07m (M1A1)

MANUFACTURER: YUGOSLAVIAN STATE ORD-
NANCE FACTORIES

BACKGROUND

Based on the Soviet T-72, the M-84 has numerous modifications to suit Yugoslavian requirements. The M-84 is thought to have improved protection, more sophisticated fire control, and greater motive power than the T-72. The M-84 project was launched in 1976, the first vehicles rolling off the production line in 1984. A product improved vehicle produced from 1988 and known as the M-84A, is the only major variant. As production of the vehicle was scattered over the now fractured, Republic of Yugoslavia, it will be difficult for any of the newly formed states in the region to produce the M-84 without outside assistance.

A further advance on the M-84 design, the V 2001 MBT, was intended to enter into production in 1996. The V 2001 has had its development disrupted by the conflict within Yugoslavia, and its prospects are uncertain.

PROTECTION

The M-84 has a similar level of protection as the T-72. The manufacturer claims a higher level of armour

A model of the proposed V2001.   *(Courtesy of the*

and improved survivability for the M-84A. It is likely that a form of laminated armour is added to the frontal arc of the tank. Evidence from the fighting within Yugoslavia, suggests that if the fighting compartment is penetrated, the M-84 remains as vulnerable to catastrophic secondary explosion as the T-72 series as a whole.

An NBC system and smoke grenade launchers are fitted as standard.

FIREPOWER

The tank has the same fully stabilised 125mm smoothbore cannon and autoloader as the T-72. Up to 44 rounds of 125mm ammunition are carried, 22 of which are installed in the autoloader. The locally produced SAV-84 fire control system appears to be more sophisticated than Russian equivalents available on the early T-72. The M-84A has a digital fire control computer. This incorporates data from a laser rangefinder which is integral to the gunner's sights, and from a rather prominent meteorological sensor mounted on the front of the turret roof. Night fighting apparatus is superior to the baseline T-72; it includes second generation image intensifiers, rather than less effective and easily detectable infra-red equipment.

MOBILITY

The M-84 has a 1,000hp diesel, a more powerful engine than that of the T-72. This gives it a better power to weight ratio and superior mobility. A torsion bar suspension is fitted.

ASSESSMENT

The M-84 is basically a product improved version of the T-72, with enhanced protection, fire control and mobility. The design is as good as any of the T-72 family. The M-84 would probably have carved out a bigger niche for itself in the market, if development and production had not been disrupted by war.

SERVICE STATUS

Croatia has 27 M-84 tanks in service. Kuwait, 150 M-84A tanks. Slovenia, 42 tanks. Yugoslavia (Serbia/

M-84   *(Courtesy of the Manufacturer)*

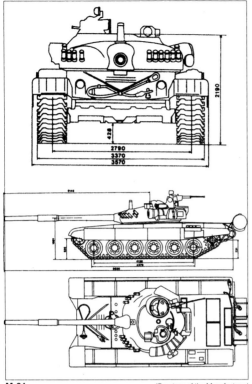

M-84

(Courtesy of the Manufacturer)

Prototype:	1982
In service:	1984
Crew:	3
Armament:	Main, 125mm smoothbore cannon. Secondary, coaxial 1 x 7.62mm MG, anti-aircraft 1 x 12.7mm MG
Combat weight:	42,000kg
Power-to-weight ratio:	23.8hp/t
Ground pressure:	0.81kg/cm^2
Length gun forward:	9.53m
Hull length:	6.86m
Hull width:	3.59m
Height (to turret roof):	2.19m
Ground clearance:	0.47m
Power pack:	Multi-fuel 12 cylinder liquid cooled diesel of 1,000hp coupled to a manual transmission
Max road speed:	65km/h
Max range (with external tanks):	700km
Fording (unprepared):	1.2m
Gradient:	60%
Side slope:	40%
Vertical obstacle:	0.85m

Montenegro), 232 M-84 tanks. Libya and Syria are each thought to have an unknown number of M-84 tanks in service.

Reconnaissance has always been one of the main functions of light tanks. As reconnaissance vehicles, their sensors and their radios are more important weapons than their cannon. Post 1945, there has been a reduction in importance of light tanks. This has been caused by three distinct factors: First, the increasing availability of specialised, airborne reconnaissance platforms, including remotely piloted vehicles. Second, many of the screening and scouting functions of Light Tanks have been taken over by wheeled armour. This has come about because of improvements in the mobility of wheeled vehicles; their tactical agility is now comparable to that of tracked ones. Wheeled armour is cheaper to run, easier to maintain, and being quieter has a reduced battlefield signature.

Third, some armies have chosen to reconnoitre a battlefield through strength rather than through stealth. The arrival of effective infantry HEAT anti-tank projectiles made light tanks too vulnerable to use in many circumstances. Instead of using light tanks, some armies will fight for information using heavy armour – pathfinding by force, rather than reconnaissance through stealth.

Yet light tanks hung on to their role, either with armies who could not afford more expensive MBTs, or for use in areas with tangled, difficult terrain where heavy, bulky, MBTs could not operate. In recent years the major powers have become more concerned with enhancing their ability to intervene rapidly in bush wars. In this changing world, the light tank has a potential new niche. This is because of their greater strategic mobility when compared to MBTs. Light tanks can be carried by air and be available at the site of a distant conflict quicker than MBTs, which have mostly to be transferred by sea.

New technology has meant the availability of lightweight, high performance armour and large calibre low-recoil weapons. It is now possible to give light tanks greater protection and a heavier punch. The use of modular armour that is both replaceable and upgradable is particularly important.

In the section on light tanks, the focus is on survivability rather than levels of protection. This is because – unlike in the case of MBTs – weight of armour is of less concern than stealth, speed and low battlefield signature.

MANUFACTURER: STEYR-DAIMLER-PUCH
SPEZIALFAHRZEUG AG

BACKGROUND

The Steyr Sk 105 (sometimes referred to as the Kürassier) was built to meet an Austrian Army requirement for a light armoured vehicle with a powerful punch capable of killing MBTs. It could be considered as a tank destroyer rather than a light tank. The requirement called for a tank light enough to maintain good mobility in terrain unsuitable for armoured operations. Development of the Steyr SK 105 began in 1965, using the strengthened hull of the Saurer APC. The tank has undergone a process of modernisation whilst in service, the original model Steyr SK 105 being supplanted by the A1 and A2 variants.

SURVIVABILITY

The basic Steyr SK 105 has armour capable of defeating 20mm cannon rounds over its frontal arc. That level of protection can be upgraded with appliqué amour kits capable of stopping 35mm rounds. The A2 variant of the tank has a re-profiled turret front giving a better ballistic shape. A variant of the tank being trialled, and not yet ordered, the A3, has greatly increased protection.

The turret of the A3 is claimed to offer the same level of protection over its frontal arc enjoyed by the turret of M48/60 MBTs.

Smoke grenades, an NBC system and an automatic fire extinguishing system are fitted as standard. As part of an upgrading package, the manufacturers offer to fit a more effective halon gas fire extinguishing system.

FIREPOWER

The tank has an oscillating turret equipped with the French 105 G1, 105mm cannon. The turret strongly resembles that of the AMX-13. Both HEAT and APFSDS rounds can be fired from the gun, the kinetic projectile being made available as part of an in service upgrade programme. In the case of both the basic Steyr SK 105 and the A1 variant, a stabilised cannon is not fitted as standard, although the A2 variant does have a stabilised weapon. In all models of the Steyr an autoloader is fitted, semi-automatic in the case of the baseline model, fully automatic in later production and renovated machines. Two revolver magazines feed the autoloader. Each of the magazines, which are situated in the turret bustle, holds six rounds. The maximum rate of fire is one round every five seconds. Up to 41 rounds are carried for the main gun. Once the small capacity magazines are empty,

SK 105 upgraded with infra-red/whte light searchlight.   *(Courtesy of Will Fowler)*

SK 105 A1 rear left view.   *(Courtesy of the Manufacturer)*

SK 105 A1 side view   *(Courtesy of the Manufacturer)*

SK 105 A2 side view.   *(Courtesy of the Manufacturer)*

the tank's crew has to reload them from outside the tank. This is a risky process on the battlefield.

Early Steyr 105 tanks had infra-red sights for night gunnery and a laser rangefinder. The A1 model has a digital fire control system and passive night sights for both commander and gunner. The A2 has an updated and more capable fire control system with a fully stabilised gun. The A3 vehicle – not yet in production – carries the M68 105mm cannon, based on the British L7 weapon.

MOBILITY

The Steyr SK 105 has a better power-to-weight ratio and a lower ground pressure than the AMX-13, despite being heavier. A torsion bar suspension is fitted; later models of the tank, or those subject to an upgrade package, have hydraulic bump stops. Basic Steyr SK 105s have a manual transmission; more recent and upgraded vehicles have a fully automatic transmission.

ASSESSMENT

The tank, although of an earlier generation, features many of the design characteristics of the more modern US AGS fighting vehicle. An autoloader, powerful weapon for the weight of tank and high agility are all noteworthy. The Steyr SK 105 was an advanced vehicle for its time, and in its latest versions is still effective.

SERVICE STATUS

Argentina has 106 of the tanks in service. Austria, 234 tanks. Bolivia, 36 tanks. Morocco 100 tanks. Tunisia 55.

Prototype:	1967
In service:	1971
Crew:	3
Armament:	Main, 105mm cannon. Secondary, coaxial 1 x 7.62mm MG, anti-aircraft 1 x 7.62mm MG
Combat weight:	17,700kg.
Power-to-weight ratio:	18.1hp/t
Ground pressure:	0.67kg/cm^2
Length gun forward:	7.76m
Hull length:	5.58m
Hull width:	2.5m
Height (to commander's cupola):	2.53m
Ground clearance:	0.4m
Power pack:	Steyr 7FA 6-cylinder, liquid-cooled, turbocharged diesel of 320hp coupled to an automatic transmission
Max road speed:	68km/h
Max range (internal fuel):	520km
Fording (unprepared):	1m
Gradient:	75%
Side slope:	40%
Vertical obstacle:	0.8m

MANUFACTURER: CHINESE STATE ORDNANCE FACTORIES

BACKGROUND

The Chinese developed the Type 62 light tank from 1958 when it became apparent that even the relatively light Type 59 tank had difficulties operating in some of China's wilder terrain. The Type 62 is a scaled down version of the Type 59.

SURVIVABILITY

The Type 62 has only a basic level of armour protection, probably proof against machine gun fire over its frontal arc. The domed, cast turret, has a better ballistic shape than the welded turret of the similar Russian PT-76.

Neither an NBC system nor smoke grenade launchers are fitted as standard, although it is likely that the tank can lay down a smoke screen by injecting fuel into its engine exhaust.

FIREPOWER

The tank carries an 85mm rifled cannon, the performance of which is none too impressive by modern standards. No details of the fire control system are available but it is likely to be basic. The tank does not carry night-fighting equipment as standard. Some Type 62 tanks may have had laser rangefinders fitted externally.

MOBILITY

The tank has a reasonably high power-to-weight ratio, and is likely to be an agile opponent in difficult terrain where heavier vehicles will flounder. Suspension is of a torsion bar type. Surprisingly – the tank being used by Chinese marines – the vehicle is not amphibious.

ASSESSMENT

The tank is a very basic fighting machine. Its utility lies in its ability to operate in harsh terrain, in which heavier and more powerful tanks would not be able to function. The tank is cheaper than most of its competitors. In addition it does not impose the heavy logistic burden that more sophisticated machines do, thus it is suitable for use by armies in developing countries.

SERVICE STATUS

In service with Albania, 30 tanks. Bangladesh, 40 tanks. China, 800 tanks. Congo, 10 tanks. Korea, North, up to 50 tanks. Mali, 18 tanks. Sudan, 70 tanks. Tanzania, 30 tanks. Vietnam, number in service unknown. Zaire, approximately 40 tanks.

Prototype:	Probably 1959-60
In service:	1962
Crew:	4
Armament:	Main, 85mm rifled cannon. Secondary, bow 1 x 7.62mm MG, coaxial 1 x 7.62mm MG, anti-aircraft 1 x 12.7 mm MG
Combat weight:	21,00kg
Power-to-weight ratio:	20.47hp/t
Ground pressure:	0.71kg/cm^2
Length gun forward:	7.9m
Hull length:	5.55m
Hull width:	2.86m
Height (to top of turret):	2.25m
Ground clearance:	0.42m
Power pack:	Liquid cooled diesel of 430hp coupled to a manual transmission
Max road speed:	60km/h
Max range (internal fuel):	500km
Fording (unprepared):	1.3m
Gradient:	60%
Side slope:	40%
Vertical obstacle:	0.7 m

MANUFACTURER: CHINESE STATE ORDNANCE
FACTORIES

BACKGROUND

The Type 63 light tank is an amphibious fighting vehicle
of the same class as – and closely based upon – the
Russian PT-76. The tank is somewhat beefier than the
PT-76, being larger, heavier and better armed.
Developed in the late 1950s, the Type 63 fills the need
that many countries have, for an agile light tank that is
cheap to buy and simple to operate.

SURVIVABILITY

The tank has an all-welded steel hull with a cast turret.
The cast turret is the main visible dissimilarity between
the Type 63 and Pt-76. The Chinese tank's dome-shaped
turret has a better ballistic shape than its Russian
competitor. Like the PT-76, the Type 63 tank has a large
volume for its light weight; this is due to the requirement
that it be fully amphibious. The obvious disadvantage of
large volume coupled to light weight, is thin armour.
Battlefield survivability is likely to be low if the vehicle is
caught in a fire fight. To compound matters the Type 63
appears not to have an NBC system.

FIREPOWER

An 85mm cannon is carried. This offers superior
firepower to the 76.6mm cannon of the PT-76, but is
bought at the cost of an even more cramped crew
compartment. The poor ergonomics of the Type 63 is
bound to eventually exhaust even the most competent
crew. Some Type 63 tanks have had their fire control
upgraded by the addition of a laser range finder mounted
externally over the rear of the main weapon. There are
no night sights fitted as standard.

North Korea has produced its own light amphibious
tank, the M 1985, which blends characteristics of the
Type 63 and the PT-76. The M 1985 has improved
firepower when compared to either the Chinese or
Russian tanks. The Korean vehicle has a mount for a
Sagger anti-tank missile, fixed above its 73mm cannon.

MOBILITY

As the Type 63 has a more powerful engine, it has a
better power-to-weight ratio than the PT-76. Suspension
is torsion bar. The vehicle is fully amphibious with minimal
preparation and is propelled through water by two water
jets.

ASSESSMENT

Cheap, simple and agile, the Type 63 meets a market
demand. However despite its agility and its amphibious
qualities, the Type 63 is easily outclassed by the new
generation of light tanks coming on the market from
Western manufacturers.

SERVICE STATUS

The tank is in service with China, 1,200 tanks. Korea,
North uses 560 light amphibious tanks, including the
PT-76, M 1985 as well as the Type 63. The exact number
of Type 63 tanks is unknown. Vietnam, 150 tanks.

Prototype:	Early 1960s
In service:	1963
Crew:	4
Armament:	Main, 85mm cannon. Secondary, coaxial 1 x 7.62mm MG, anti-aircraft 1 x 12.7mm MG
Combat weight:	18,700kg
Power-to-weight ratio:	21.39hp/t
Ground pressure:	Not available
Length gun forward:	8.44m
Hull length:	7.15m
Hull width:	3.2m
Height (to turret top):	2.52m
Ground clearance:	0.4m
Power pack:	Model 12150-L water cooled diesel of 400hp coupled to a manual transmission
Max road speed:	64km/h. (12km/h in water)
Max range (internal fuel):	370km
Fording:	Amphibious
Gradient:	60%
Side slope:	30%
Vertical obstacle:	0.87m

MANUFACTURER: GIAT INDUSTRIES

BACKGROUND
The AMX-13 began life as a design project in 1946 and entered into production in 1952. Now approaching the end of its useful life, the AMX-13 has seen combat and proved a useful fighting machine.

The basic chassis of the AMX-13 has been used as the basis for a whole family of armoured vehicles, including an infantry fighting vehicle, self-propelled guns and anti-aircraft guns.

SURVIVABILITY
The AMX-13 has thin armour of all-welded steel, and has limited survivability when faced by heavier equipment. The AMX-13 relies on its speed and agility to keep itself out of harms way. In recent years the original manufacturer and several competitors have offered various add-on armour packages.

FIREPOWER
All AMX-13 variants have a unique, oscillating turret. The upper half of the turret carrying the main gun, swivels up and down to bring the main armament to bear. The main armament is fed by an autoloader linked to two magazines, each with six ready to use shells. Additional ammunition is stored in the hull, and rather vulnerably, in the turret.

The original weapon fit was a 75mm gun; later models of the AMX-13 were fitted with 90mm cannon. Many of the early tanks have been up-gunned with this weapon. A further firepower upgrade involving a 105mm cannon has not been widely adopted. The original fire control system was rather basic. More modern systems involving laser range-finders and digital computers have been offered by several companies.

MOBILITY
With impressive mobility when first put into service, the standard AMX-13 now looks a little dated. The manufacturer has offered a new build machine on the market, the AMX-13 Version 1987. This has a new diesel engine, transmission and suspension, which greatly improve performance. Torsion bar suspension is fitted as standard.

AMX-13 front left view.   *(Copyright of Marsh Gelbart)*

135

ASSESSMENT

A successful design with some unique features, the AMX-13 is long in the tooth, but until the new generation of light tanks are more widely available, the AMX-13 will remain viable. The AMX-13 Version 1987 offers substantial improvements in combat effectiveness.

SERVICE STATUS

Argentina has 58 tanks in service. Dominica, 12 tanks. Ecuador, 108 tanks. Indonesia, 275 tanks. Ivory Coast, 5 tanks. Lebanon, 30 tanks. Peru, 110 tanks. Singapore is the main user of the AMX-13 with 350 tanks; it has introduced so many improvements that its version has its own entry. Venezuela, 36 tanks.

AMX-13 In Israeli service with 75 mm gun, front right view.
(Copyright of Marsh Gelbart)

(90mm version)

Prototype:	1948
In service:	1953
Crew:	3
Armament:	Main, 90mm. Secondary, coaxial, 1 x 7.62mm MG, anti-aircraft 1 x 7.62mm MG
Combat weight:	15,000
Power-to-weight ratio:	16.66hp/t
Ground pressure:	0.76kg/cm²
Length gun forward:	6.36m
Hull length:	4.88m
Hull width:	2.51m
Height (to top of commanders hatch):	2.3m
Ground clearance:	0.37m
Power pack:	SOFAM Model 8Gxb petrol engine of 250hp
Max road speed:	60km/h
Max range (internal fuel):	350km
Fording (unprepared):	0.6m
Gradient:	60%
Side slope:	60%
Vertical obstacle:	0.65m

MANUFACTURER: THYSSEN HENSCHEL

BACKGROUND

In many ways the JPz 4-5 is an anachronism. It does not have a turret but is a casemate design with its main armament, pintle mounted, behind thick frontal armour. It is a tracked tank destroyer, dependent on its cannon to kill enemy armour. Such vehicles are a vanishing breed as missile carriers have taken over the role. The JPz 4-5 is included as it represented the best of a class of fighting vehicles that has been left behind by advances in military technology.

A series of prototypes were built by Thyssen and Hanomag from 1961. The vehicle was accepted in service in 1965.

SURVIVABILITY

As the JPz 4-5 does not have a turret, it has an exceptionally low silhouette. This helps to minimise its battlefield signature and enhances chances of survival. The lack of a turret allows additional weight to be allocated to armouring the well-shaped front of the vehicle. As the crew's fighting compartment is at the front

and the power pack at the rear, the extra armour is a desirable feature. Armour is made up of an all-welded steel shell.

Smoke grenades, an NBC system, and automatic fire extinguishing equipment for the engine compartment, are fitted as standard.

FIREPOWER

The JPz 4-5 carries a 90mm cannon (a 105mm cannon can be fitted but is not mounted as standard), in a ball-type mount. The gun is able to elevate to plus 15 degrees and be depressed to minus 8 degrees. The ball mounting allows a limited ability to traverse 15 degrees to the left and 15 degrees to the right. Some 51 rounds of 90mm ammunition are stowed. Sights and fire control are basic as befits the vintage of the vehicle. Night fighting sights are infra-red. Belgium purchased the JPz 4-5 and fitted a more sophisticated fire control system, which uses an analogue computer and laser rangefinder as fitted to Belgium's Leopard 1. Whilst a 90mm cannon may have been adequate as a weapon at the time of the vehicle's inception, it is no longer able to meet modern threat levels. The main reason why the casemate design has

Jagdpanzer Kanone showing its low profile.   *(Courtesy of the Manufacturer)*

become obsolete, is that advances in fire control systems have undermined the validity of fixed or semi-fixed cannon designs. Modern electronics allow MBTs to fire on the move at moving targets with a good chance of a kill. The JPz 4-5 was built to stalk enemy armour and fire whilst stationary. It has been left behind by the potential pace of the modern battlefield.

MOBILITY

The vehicle's transmission and torsion bar suspension are similar to those of the Marder infantry fighting vehicle. The first, second, fourth and fifth wheel stations have hydraulic shock absorbers. The JPz 4-5 is an agile vehicle with what for its time was a high power-to-weight ratio.

ASSESSMENT

Although the cannon armed tank destroyer may have been replaced by the missile armed tank killer, the JPz 4-5 was a sound design for its time. Of the 770 JPz 4-5 tank destroyers built, many were converted to carry a HOT or TOW missile launcher rather than a cannon as their main armament.

SERVICE STATUS

Belgium has withdrawn the JPz 4-5 from service. Germany has eight of the cannon-armed variant in service plus 258 HOT missile armed conversions, and 142 of the TOW armed versions.

Prototype:	1960
In service:	1965
Crew:	4
Armament:	Main 90mm rifled cannon. Secondary, coaxial 1 x 7.62mm MG, anti-aircraft 1 x 7.62mm MG
Combat weight:	27,500kg
Power-to-weight ratio:	18.18hp/t
Ground pressure:	0.75kg/cm²
Length gun forward:	8.75m
Hull length:	6.24m
Hull width:	2.98m
Height (to turret top):	2.08m
Ground clearance:	0.44m
Power pack:	Daimler Benz MB 837 8 cylinder water cooled diesel of 500hp coupled to a hydrostatic transmission
Max road speed:	70km/h
Max range (internal fuel):	450km
Fording (unprepared):	1.2m
Gradient:	58%
Side slope:	30%
Vertical obstacle:	0.75m

MANUFACTURER: GIAT INDUSTRIES/HÄGGLUNDS VEHICLE

BACKGROUND

This tank, aimed at the export market, combines the hull of the Swedish CV 90 IFV with a turret developed by Giat of France. For its class it has a good blend of protection, firepower and mobility. The vehicle completed trials in 1994, but so far it has not received any orders.

SURVIVABILITY

The vehicle, like the CV 90 IFV, has its engine at the front, the driver being seated at the front left. This helps to improve crew survivability as the mass of the power pack helps shield the crew compartment should the frontal armour be pierced. The hull is made out of all-welded steel, and over its frontal arc, is likely to cope with light cannon rounds of up to approximately 25mm calibre. The turret is proof against heavy calibre machine gun fire.

As far as other measures affecting survivability go, the tank is claimed to have a reduced infra-red signature, and has smoke grenades and an NBC system as standard. Additional armour can be fitted at a customer's discretion as can a fire detection/suppression system.

FIREPOWER

The CV 90105 TML mounts the French G2 rifled cannon. This has the same ballistic characteristics as the widely used British L7 weapon, therefore increasing the choice of ammunition supply. Stabilisation of the gun is optional, dependent on customer requirements. If the customer wishes, the TML turret can mount a selection of alternate weapons, other than the G2 cannon. Some 40 rounds are carried for the main gun, 12 in the turret. As the tank has a rear door – like the Israeli Merkava MBT – ammunition replenishment should be easier than usual. Up to four infantry men can be carried in a somewhat confined space at the hull rear.

Fire control is sophisticated, the gunner having thermal night sights and laser rangefinder. Vehicle optics are filtered to protect the crew against eye damage from battlefield lasers.

MOBILITY

The tank has a high power-to-weight ratio and a low

CV 90 105 TML light tank.   *(Courtesy of the Manufacturer)*

ground pressure. A torsion bar suspension is fitted with rotary dampers. The driver can adjust track tension from within the vehicle.

ASSESSMENT
The CV 90105 TML is a sophisticated European effort waiting its chance to force its way into the light tank market. The machines front mounted engine is an interesting and useful feature.

CV 90 105 TML light tank.   *(Courtesy of the Manufacturer)*

SERVICE STATUS
Not yet in service, awaiting orders.

Prototype:	1994
In service:	Not yet in service
Crew:	4 (The vehicle can carry 4 infantrymen in its rear compartment)
Armament:	Main, 105mm rifled cannon. Secondary, 1 x 7.62mm MG
Combat weight:	22,500kg
Power-to-weight ratio:	27hp/t
Ground pressure:	0.51kg/cm²
Length gun forward:	8.8m
Hull length:	6.5m
Hull width:	3.1m
Height (to turret roof):	2.34m
Ground clearance:	0.45m
Power pack:	Scania DS114 diesel of 606hp coupled to an automatic transmission
Max road speed:	70km/h
Max range:	Not available
Fording:	Not available
Gradient:	60%
Side slope:	40%
Vertical obstacle:	1.2m

MANUFACTURER: SOVIET STATE FACTORIES

BACKGROUND
The PT-76 was developed at the end of the Second World War to provide an amphibious reconnaissance capability for Soviet armoured forces. Built between 1952 and the late 1960s, the PT-76 has seen widespread service.

SURVIVABILITY
The PT-76 has thin, all-welded steel armour. It can be penetrated by heavy machine gun fire. The amphibious requirement dictated a design that was both large and lightweight. This led to poor survivability on the battlefield. Rudimentary NBC protection and minimal night fighting equipment, have not helped battlefield durability.

PT-76 Light Amphibious Tank. *(Courtesy of Will Fowler)*

PT-76 from the front. *(Copyright of Marsh Gelbart)*

Damaged PT-76. Note that the tracks have been torn off and the turret pierced by weapons fire. *(Copyright of Marsh Gelbart)*

FIREPOWER
Firepower is at best adequate. The initial PT-76 carried a D-56T 76mm gun; newer models of the tank mount a gun with an improved muzzle brake and bore evacuator. Late variants of the tank, known as the PT-76B, have a fully stabilised gun system.

MOBILITY
The PT-76's light weight and amphibious ability, allow it to scout and skirmish across terrain that would deter heavier, more powerful, fighting vehicles. Suspension is torsion bar. The tank is powered through water by two water jets situated at the rear of the hull. The only other preparation required when the tank takes to water is to raise a frontal trim vane and switch on the bilge pumps.

ASSESSMENT
The PT-76, despite its poor survivability, remains viable on the battlefield. This is because of its amphibious mobility. The vehicle is likely to remain useful until a new generation of light tanks comes into service.

China has produced a more powerful variant – see the entry for the Type 63, whilst an Israeli company NIMDA, has upgraded the basic PT-76. The NIMDA vehicle has major improvements to its firepower and mobility, but it has not yet been ordered.

SERVICE STATUS
The PT-76 is in widespread service within the borders of the old Soviet Union and its political allies. In many of the armies where the PT-76 remains in service, they are poorly maintained, and of dubious combat effectiveness.

Afghanistan has 60 tanks. Angola, 10 tanks. Benin, 20 tanks. Cambodia, 10 tanks. CIS, 200 tanks. Congo, 3 tanks. Cuba, 50 tanks. Guinea, 20 tanks. Guinea-Bissau, 20 tanks. Indonesia, 30 tanks. Korea (North), exact figures unknown but probably several hundred. Laos, 25 tanks. Madagascar, 12 tanks. Nicaragua, 22 tanks. Poland, 30 tanks. Vietnam, 250 tanks. Zambia 30 tanks.

Prototype:	1952
In service:	1955
Crew:	3
Armament:	Main, 1 x 76.2mm cannon. Secondary, coaxial 1 x 7.62mm MG
Combat weight:	14,000kg
Power-to-weight ratio:	17.1hp/t
Ground pressure:	0.479kg/cm^2
Length gun forward:	7.625m
Hull length:	6.91m
Hull width:	3.14m
Height (to top of turret):	2.255m
Ground clearance:	0.37m
Power pack:	Model V6, 6-cylinder in-line diesel of 240hp, coupled to a manual transmission
Max speed:	44km/h (10km/h in water)
Max range (internal fuel):	280km road, 65km water
Fording:	Amphibious
Gradient:	70%
Side slope:	40%
Vertical obstacle:	1.1m

MANUFACTURER: SINGAPORE AUTOMOTIVE ENGINEERING

BACKGROUND

Singapore is the major remaining user of the AMX-13 light tank, the vehicle being well suited for local terrain. In the late 1980s Singapore decided to launch a major upgrade of the AMX-13 design, concentrating on the vehicle's power train and running gear.

SURVIVABILITY

Passive protection remains that of the baseline AMX-13, however battlefield survivability is likely to be enhanced by the vehicles increased speed, and in particular by its improved acceleration. The replacement of the original petrol engine with a diesel means that the tank is less likely to catch fire if hit.

FIREPOWER

Firepower remains the same as that of the AMX-13.

MOBILITY

The main changes from the AMX-13 are in the field of mobility. The AMX-13 SM1 has a new diesel engine, an automatic transmission, and an advanced hydropneumatic suspension system. The suspension has greater wheel travel than the original torsion bar suspension, 275mm from static to bump stop, compared to the torsion bar system's 115mm. This allows for enhanced shock absorption and enables the tank to make full use of its improved power-to-weight ratio. The combination of increased power and superior suspension, gives greater agility and acceleration, increased reliability and range plus a smoother cross-country ride.

ASSESSMENT

Singapore has produced an enhanced version of an obsolescent tank. In its new guise the vehicle should be able to give sterling service at a fraction of the cost of a new purchase. The manufacturers are offering similar modifications in kit form for other countries' AMX-13s.

SERVICE STATUS

Only in service with Singapore, which has up to 350 baseline vehicles converted to AMX-13 SM1 standards.

(All specifications are the same as the AMX-13 (qv) except for those features listed below)

Prototype:	1986/7
In service:	1988
Power-to-weight ratio:	19hp/t
Power pack:	Detroit Diesel 6V-53T engine of 290hp coupled to an automatic transmission
Max road speed:	64km/h
Max range (internal fuel):	450/500km

MANUFACTURER: HÄGGLUNDS VEHICLE AB

BACKGROUND

Strictly speaking the Infanterikanonvagn 91 (Ikv-91) is a tank destroyer rather than a light tank. Rather than being a fighting vehicle intended primarily for reconnaissance, the Ikv-91 is intended to give an anti-tank capability to light mechanised forces operating in an Arctic environment. The design of the Ikv-91 dates back to the early 1970s; the first Ikv-91 entered into Swedish service in 1975.

SURVIVABILITY

The main design priorities of the Ikv-91 are firepower and mobility rather than protection, yet its careful layout assists crew survivability. The turret and hull are of all welded steel; the frontal arc of the Ikv is intended to survive hits from light cannon up to 20mm in calibre. The hull sides are doubled skinned, with diesel fuel stored in the resultant available space. Much of the fuel is thus incorporated in a form of spaced armour, helping to protect the crew. Smoke grenades and flare launchers are carried as standard, as is an NBC system.

FIREPOWER

The Ikv-91 mounts a 90mm low pressure cannon, this relies on fin stabilised HEAT projectile to kill enemy tanks. The gun is not stabilised, but is fitted with a thermal shroud. Of the 59 rounds of 90mm ammunition carried, 16 are ready rounds stored at the loader's station.

Fire control and optics are reasonably comprehensive, but do not include night vision systems. Gun laying incorporates a laser rangefinder in the gunner's sight. Not all input to the ballistic computer is fully automatic, meteorological conditions have to be entered manually.

MOBILITY

The Ikv-91 is a fighting vehicle specifically designed to function in the harsh terrain and climate of Scandinavia. It has a good power-to-weight ratio, and low ground pressure, both particularly important given the operating conditions. The tank is amphibious, given minimal preparation, a useful characteristic with the large number of lakes in Sweden's territory.

Suspension is of the torsion bar type; hydraulic shock absorbers are fitted to the first and last wheel

Hagglund Vehicle Infanterikanonvagn 91 Tank Destroyer showing its sleek silhouette and low profile. *(Courtesy of the Manufacturer)*

stations. The tracks can be fitted with studs or spikes to increase traction on snow or ice.

ASSESSMENT
The Ikv-91 carries a powerful gun on a light chassis. At the time of its inception it was a well-armed vehicle, nowadays several other light fighting vehicles – even including some wheeled ones – carry at least as heavy an armament. The Ikv-91 was a well thought out design for a particular environment. Today it is still a competent fighting vehicle, but is beginning to look a little dated.

SERVICE STATUS
Sweden has 210 Ivk-91 tank destroyers in service.

Prototype:	1969
In service:	1975
Crew:	4
Armament:	Main, 90mm low pressure gun. Secondary, 1 x 7.62 mm MG, anti-aircraft 1 x 7.62 mm MG
Combat weight:	16,300kg
Power-to-weight ratio:	22.2hp/t
Ground pressure:	0.49kg/cm^2
Length gun forward:	8.84m
Hull length:	6.41m
Hull width:	3.0m
Height (to commander's cupola):	2.32 m
Ground clearance:	0.37m
Power pack:	Volvo-Penta TD 120 6-cylinder turbocharged diesel of 330hp coupled to an automatic transmission
Max road speed:	65km/h. In water the tank is driven by its tracks at 6.5km/h
Max range (internal fuel):	500km
Fording:	Amphibious with minimal preparation
Gradient:	60%
Side slope:	40%
Vertical obstacle:	0.8m

MANUFACTURER: ALVIS LIMITED

BACKGROUND
Scimitar is based on the Combat Vehicle Reconnaissance (Tracked) family. Scimitar resembles the Scorpion light tank, sharing the same hull and turret, but with a different weapons fit. The machine is a reconnaissance vehicle relying on skill, stealth and speed rather than brawn, to obtain information on the enemy. Developed in 1971, Scimitar went into service in 1973.

SURVIVABILITY
The Scimitar has a body shell and turret made of aluminium armour, which offers protection against heavy machine gun fire over the vehicles frontal arc. The sides and rear of the vehicle are protected against shrapnel and light arms fire. The job of the Scimitar is to obtain information, avoid contact and to report, not to get into a stand-up fight. It is fitted with smoke grenade dischargers to screen its movements.

FIREPOWER
Scimitar is fitted with the very effective and accurate 30mm Rarden cannon. This can take out most light armour that the Scimitar is likely to encounter, and offers a potent weapon against bunkers. The Rarden usually fires rapid, aimed, single shots; however it can fire bursts of six rounds. The secondary armament, a 7.62 mm machine gun, is of use against infantry in the open. Passive image intensifying night sights are fitted.

MOBILITY
The vehicle has a high power-to-weight ratio and is agile. Travelling in Scimitar at speed over rough terrain is quite an experience! The suspension is of a torsion bar type. Hydraulic shock absorbers are fitted to the first and last pair of road wheels. The baseline power pack is a petrol engine. It would not be technically difficult to replace this with a more powerful diesel as is on offer with Scorpion.Scimitar is easily air portable.

ASSESSMENT
The Scimitar is a fine vehicle for carrying out a specific function. It has not sold as well as Scorpion, but is probably a better vehicle for the reconnaissance role.

Scimitar in a Bosnian Winter. *(Courtesy of the Manufacturer)*

SERVICE STATUS

Belgium has 153 Scimitars in service and 33 in storage. Honduras has a handful of Scimitars in service. Approximately 315 are in service with the British Armed Forces.

Prototype:	1971
In service:	1973
Crew:	3
Armament:	Main, 30mm Rarden cannon. Secondary, coaxial 1 x 7.62 mm MG
Combat weight:	7,800kg
Power-to-weight ratio:	24.5hp/t
Ground pressure:	0.338kg/cm^2
Length gun forward:	4.985m
Hull length:	4.79m
Hull width:	2.242m
Height:	2.096m
Ground clearance:	0.42 m
Power pack:	Jaguar J60 No1 Mk 100B petrol engine of 190hp
Max road speed:	80km/h
Max range (internal fuel):	644km
Fording (unprepared):	1.067m
Gradient:	60%
Vertical obstacle:	0.5m

Scimitar in the mud. *(Copyright of Marsh Gelbart)*

Scimitar and crew at rest. Turret turned to the right. Note the vehicle is fitted with weapon simulatrors for training purposes. *(Copyright of Marsh Gelbart)*

Scimitars awaiting the order to move. Note the vehicle is fitted with weapon simulators for training puroposes.

(Copyright of Marsh Gelbart)

MANUFACTURER: ALVIS VEHICLES LTD

BACKGROUND

Strictly speaking the Scorpion is really a reconnaissance vehicle rather than a light tank. However its configuration lends its use as a light tank, particularly when used in internal security scenarios, or in the service of the armed forces of developing countries. The Scorpion like the Scimitar (see relevant entry), is a member of a family of armoured vehicles built by Alvis. The different members of the family use common components wherever possible to minimise costs and simplify maintenance.

The Scorpion itself was developed from the mid 1960s to meet a requirement for a tracked reconnaissance vehicle. Entering into service in 1970, the Scorpion has been widely sold and undergone many improvements in service.

SURVIVABILITY

Given the vehicle's light weight and thin armour, the vehicle obviously depends on speed and stealth for survival on the battlefield. The Scorpion has all aluminium armour which gives protection against 14.7mm machine gun fire over its frontal arc and 7.62 mm calibre rounds over the rest of the vehicle. An NBC system is fitted according to customer requirements, and smoke grenade launchers as standard. As part of its comprehensive upgrading package – the Scorpion Improvement Programme – Alvis offers to fit fire suppression systems.

FIREPOWER

The original weapon carried by the Scorpion, a 76mm cannon, gives the Scorpion a useful, if slightly dated, safeguard against other light armour. Many export Scorpions, known as Scorpion 90, are fitted with the more powerful Belgian Cockerill 90mm gun. Unlike the basic Scorpion, the Scorpion 90 has powered turret traverse and gun elevation. The standard Scorpion can carry 40 rounds of 76mm ammunition; the Scorpion 90 has 34 rounds for its cannon.

Fire control systems vary in complexity from user to user. Early Scorpions had rather basic fire control and

optics. More sophisticated systems incorporating day/night sights for the commander and gunner plus a laser rangefinder for the gunner are available. These can either be installed on new build machines, or be retrofitted by Alvis.

MOBILITY

The vehicle is air transportable giving strategic mobility and it has excellent battlefield agility. Scorpion's power-to-weight ratio is high and its ground pressure is low. The Scorpion carries a flotation screen; after a few minutes of preparation the vehicle becomes fully amphibious, driving itself through the water with its tracks. Floatation screens have been removed from British vehicles. All variants of the Scorpion have torsion bar suspension.

As part of the Scorpion Improvement Programme, a 200hp diesel is an optional replacement for the existing 190hp petrol engine.

ASSESSMENT

The Scorpion has been highly successful although the basic vehicle is becoming dated. The British army has withdrawn its 76mm cannon armed Scorpions, replacing

Scorpion 90 on parade in Malaysia.   *(Courtesy of Manufacturer)*

Scorpion 90 in service with Malaysia.   *(Courtesy of Manufacturer)*

them with the Sabre light armoured vehicle. Sabre mates the hull of the Scorpion, to the turret of the Fox armoured car armed with a Rarden 30mm cannon. Other countries have chosen a 90mm cannon to replace the obsolescent 76mm weapon.

One problem that came to light during the Gulf war was that the image intensification sights of the Scorpion were out-ranged by the thermal sights of Challenger MBTs. In order to act as a reconnaissance screen for modern armour, Scorpion needs to be fitted with thermal sights.

SERVICE STATUS

Belgium has 132 of 701 Scorpions remaining in service. Botswana, 36 tanks. Brunei, 16 tanks. Chile, 30 tanks in process of delivery. Honduras, 12 tanks. Iran, 80 tanks. Indonesia, 26 tanks in service plus an unknown number on order. Ireland, 14 tanks. Jordan, 19 tanks. Malaysia, 26 tanks. New Zealand, 26 tanks. Nigeria, 100 tanks. Oman, 37 tanks. Philippines, 41 tanks. Spain, 17 tanks. Tanzania, 40 tanks. Thailand, 154 tanks. Togo, 9 tanks. UAE, 76 tanks. UK, 13 tanks plus 194 in store. Venezuela, about 50 tanks.

Scorpion training with the 2nd Royal Tank Regiment in Germany. *(Courtesy of Will Fowler)*

(Information in brackets relates to Scorpion 90)

Prototype:	1969
In service:	1972
Crew:	3
Armament:	Main, 76mm rifled cannon (90mm rifled cannon)
Combat weight:	8,073kg (8,723kg)
Power-to-weight ratio:	23.54hp/t (22.92hp/t)
Ground pressure:	0.36kg/cm^2 (0.37kg/cm^2)
Length gun forward:	Not available for basic Scorpion (5.29m)
Hull length:	4.79m
Hull width:	2.23m
Height (to commander's cupola):	2.10m
Ground clearance:	0.37m (0.42 m)
Power pack:	Jaguar J 60 No 1 Mk 100B 4.2 6 cylinder petrol engine of 190hp (Perkins diesel of 200hp) coupled to a semi-automatic transmission
Max road speed:	80.5km/h (72.5km/h)
Max range (internal fuel):	644km (756km)
Fording (unprepared):	1.067m. Fully amphibious with minimal preparation
Gradient:	60%
Side slope:	40%
Vertical obstacle:	0.5m

MANUFACTURER: CADILLAC MOTOR CAR DIVISION OF GENERAL MOTORS

BACKGROUND

A sound design dating back to 1951, the M41 although obsolete, remains in service with several countries. These states have either a limited military budget or difficult terrain that restricts the use of heavier armour.

Several users of the tank have carried out extensive renovation of the basic vehicle.

SURVIVABILITY

The hull is of all-welded construction and the hull of mixed welded and cast fabrication. Despite the good ballistic shape of the front and sides of the turret and hull, armour protection is not comparable with the latest technology.

Danish M41s have been rebuilt to a new standard known as the M41 DK-1 and are fitted with side skirts, smoke grenade launchers and an NBC system to improve their survivability.

Taiwan has manufactured a small number of new build tanks known as the Type 64 and has also comprehensively rebuilt many of their M41 tanks to the same standard. The Type 64 has some ergonomic modifications making them easier to crew with soldiers of small stature. The Type 64's hull is constructed with an improved high hardness steel and has appliqué armour of a similar material attached to its turret and hull.

FIREPOWER

The original weapon fitted to the M41 was the M32 76mm rifled cannon. Fire control consisted of basic optics. For its time this was a satisfactory weapon fit, although some users have felt it necessary to up-gun their M41s; there are several upgrades available on the market.

Brazil has fitted many of its M41s either with the Belgium 90mm Cockrill gun, or an M32 cannon re-bored to 90mm. Brazil has also installed improved fire control incorporating laser rangefinding. Uruguay has also fitted the Belgian 90mm cannon. Denmark and Taiwan have fitted improved fire controls to their M41s. Danish M 41 Dk-1 light tanks and the Taiwanese M41 carry a modern round for their 76mm cannon which gives them an improved armour piercing capability.

M41 Light tank and crew.   *(Courtesy of the Tank Museum)*

MOBILITY

The original power pack was a 500hp petrol engine. In late variants of the M41 (the M41A3), the engine is fitted with fuel injection but has the same power output. Many users, including Brazil, Denmark and Taiwan, have felt it necessary to replace the standard engine. They have installed less vulnerable, and less fuel hungry, diesel power packs. Power-to-weight ratios are reasonable, even with the initial power pack. Suspension is of the torsion bar type, with hydraulic shock absorbers for the first, second and fifth pairs of road wheels.

ASSESSMENT

The tank was a well-designed package when first built. It is now showing its age and is in need of comprehensive upgrading or replacement.

SERVICE STATUS

In service with Brazil 296 tanks. Chile, 60 tanks. Denmark, 53 tanks. Dominican Republic, 12 tanks. Guatemala, 10 tanks. Taiwan, 675 (some converted to Type 64 standard). Thailand, 250 tanks, most in storage. Uruguay, 22 tanks.

Prototype:	1949
In service:	1951
Crew:	4
Armament:	Main, 76mm rifled cannon. Secondary, coaxial 1 x 7.62 mm MG, anti-aircraft 1 x 12.7mm MG
Combat weight:	23,495kg
Power-to-weight ratio:	21.62hp/t
Ground pressure:	0.72kg/cm²
Length gun forward:	8.21m
Hull length:	5.82 m
Hull width:	3.2 m
Height (to commander's cupola):	2.73m
Ground clearance:	0.45m
Power pack:	Continental AOS-895-3 6 cylinder supercharged, air-cooled petrol engine of 500hp. Late model M41s had fuel injection. In either case the power output is 500hp linked to a manual transmission
Max road speed:	72km/h
Max range (internal fuel):	161km
Fording (unprepared):	1.01m
Gradient:	60%
Side slope:	30%
Vertical obstacle:	0.71m

MANUFACTURER: ALLISON DIVISION OF GENERAL MOTORS

BACKGROUND
Introduced in 1966, the M551 was intended as the main reconnaissance platform for US ground forces. The vehicle was technologically innovative with its combined gun/missile launcher and aluminium armour. However numerous technical failings, particularly with the tank's power pack and running gear, saw it removed from the reconnaissance role in 1978. At present the M551 is relegated to providing light armour support for the US 82nd Airborne Division. Surplus M551s have been visibly modified to take on the role of aggressor force vehicles at the US National Training centre.

SURVIVABILITY
The M551 has an all-welded aluminium hull and a welded steel turret. Fighting in Vietnam demonstrated weaknesses in the vehicle's protection; it proved vulnerable to the RPG series of infantry anti-tank weapons.

NBC protection is fitted as standard. A fire suppression system is fitted but does not function automatically.

FIREPOWER
The tank is fitted with the 152mm M81 gun/missile launcher. This weapon can either fire a cumbersome conventional round with a combustible cartridge case, or the Shillelagh anti-tank missile. When the tank fires its main weapon, it suffers from severe recoil. This tends to disrupt the M551's fire control system, slowing down the rate of fire. The M551 lacks a kinetic energy tank killer, as both its conventional anti-tank rounds and the Shillelagh missile have a HEAT warhead. The use of reactive armour means that many armoured vehicles are less vulnerable to HEAT projectiles.

Both the gunner and driver have had their basic infra-red night vision sights replaced by thermal imaging; the gunner's thermal sight is that of the M60A3. Many M551s have also had a laser rangefinder retro-fitted at the commander's station.

MOBILITY
The M551 appears rather under-powered in comparison with more modern armoured vehicles. It has a diesel engine of 300hp and a torsion bar suspension. Originally designed to be fully amphibious without preparation, the

Sheridan Light Tank visually modified to resemble a Soviet ASU Assault Gun and used by the US army at Fort Irwin.

(Courtesy of Will Fowler)

Sheridan requires its floatation screen to be raised before it enters water. Once in water, the tank powers itself with its tracks.

The M551 has excellent strategic mobility being easily air portable. Indeed the M551 was amongst the first armour to arrive in Saudi Arabia, in response to the Iraqi invasion of Kuwait in 1990.

ASSESSMENT

The M551 Sheridan was never a particularly effective fighting vehicle. Although initial difficulties with its power pack and running gear were largely overcome, problems remained. Its sophisticated weapon system is too complex and lacks a kinetic energy projectile.

The M551 will remain in use until the AGS enters into service.

SERVICE STATUS

Only used by the United States. Approximately 120 remain in active service. Some 300 visually modified M551s are used to represent enemy vehicles in training exercises.

Prototype:	1961
In service:	1966
Crew:	4
Armament:	Main, 152 mm M81 gun/missile launcher. Secondary, 1 x 7.62 mm MG, anti-aircraft 1 x 12.7mm MG
Combat weight:	15,830kg
Power-to-weight ratio:	18.95hp/t
Ground pressure:	0.49kg/cm^2
Length gun forward:	not available
Hull length:	6.23m
Hull width:	2.82m
Height (to turret roof):	2.27m
Ground clearance:	0.48m
Power pack:	Detroit Diesel Model 6V-53T 6 cylinder water cooled supercharged diesel of 300hp
Max road speed:	70km/h
Max speed in water:	5.8km/h
Max range (internal fuel):	600km
Fording:	Amphibious with flotation screen
Gradient:	60%
Side slope:	40%
Vertical obstacle:	0.84m

MANUFACTURER: CADILLAC GAGE

BACKGROUND

The Stingray was designed primarily for export. As the M41 became obsolete, there was a niche in the market that the manufacturers (now Textron Marine & Land Systems), hoped to fill. Stingray has the best attributes of light armour, including an extremely high level of tactical mobility and strategic mobility – the vehicle is easily air portable. The concept was worked upon from the late 1970s; actual production began in 1988.

SURVIVABILITY

The tank has a fairly basic level of armoured protection, as expected in the case of light armour. The hull and turret are made of steel. The frontal arc of the vehicle offers protection against heavy machine gun fire, while the rest of the vehicle can survive armour piercing 7.62 mm rounds. There has been some research into adding appliqué armour including reactive explosive armour.

Special care has been taken to maximise chances of battlefield survival. The engines thermal signature has been reduced. Smoke grenade launchers are fitted, and there is the option of installing equipment allowing the tank to lay a smoke screen from its engine exhaust. A fire detection/suppression system is fitted; NBC protection is optional.

FIREPOWER

The tank mounts a British designed weapon, the Low Recoil Force 105mm cannon. This weapon fitted with a muzzle brake and other features to reduce recoil force, offers a punch disproportionate to the weight of the Stingray. Stowage is provided for 32 rounds and care is taken to store them below the turret. The digital fire control system is built by Marconi. The sophistication of the commander's and gunner's sights is dependent on the purchaser's budget; laser rangefinding is an option. A cannon muzzle reference system, to increase accuracy, is standard.

MOBILITY

The Stingray has a transversely mounted diesel that gives a high power-to-weight ratio. The torsion bar suspension is based on that of the heavier M109 self-

154
Stingray 1 shows its elegant lines.   *(Courtesy of Manufacturer)*

propelled gun. This means that the tank can cope with any future increases in weight.

ASSESSMENT
Stingray has an acceptable level of protection, a surprisingly heavy punch for a vehicle of its weight, and excellent mobility. It is a design that deserves to have sold better. Improvements to its basic level of protection would help its export prospects.

SERVICE STATUS
Only used by Thailand, 106 in service.

Prototype:	1984
In service:	1988
Crew:	4
Armament:	Main 1 x 105mm rifled, low recoil force cannon. Secondary, coaxial 1 x 7.62 mm MG, anti-aircraft 1 x 12.7mm MG
Combat weight:	21,025kg
Power-to-weight ratio:	25.93hp/t
Ground pressure:	0.72kg/cm^2
Length gun forward:	9.35m
Hull length:	6.44m
Hull width:	2.71m
Height:	2.55m
Ground clearance:	0.46m
Power pack:	Detroit Diesel Model 8V-92TA of 550hp coupled to an automatic transmission
Max road speed:	71km/h
Max range (internal fuel):	450km
Fording (unprepared):	1.07m
Gradient:	60%
Side slope:	40%
Vertical obstacle:	0.84m

MANUFACTURER: CADILLAC GAGE

BACKGROUND

The Stingray II (now manufactured by Textron Marine and Land Systems), is a direct evolution of the original Stingray design and closely resembles it. The vehicle's changes are largely in the realms of survivability. The first prototype was nearing completion in 1995.

SURVIVABILITY

The Stingray II has better ballistic protection than its predecessor. A spaced armour configuration, using high hardness steel plate, allows all-round protection against heavy machine gun fire. An optional appliqué passive armour package, gives protection against infantry light anti-tank weapons over the vehicle's frontal arc.

There is an option to replace the original electro-hydraulic gun control system with an all-electric one, thus reducing the risk of burns to the crew in case of battle damage.

FIREPOWER

The tank mounts the same weapon as the original Stingray, however it has more sophisticated gun laying. The Marconi fire control system has been upgraded and linked to more sophisticated crew sights. These include a Hughes day/night sight with a thermal imager for the gunner, complete with a remote display for the tank commander.

MOBILITY

The Stingray II retains the same engine as the earlier variant of the tank, along with an upgraded transmission. As the Stingray II is slightly heavier than its predecessor, there has been a marginal reduction in its power-to-weight ratio. As an alternative to the standard power pack, the manufacturer offers to install an enhanced version.

ASSESSMENT

If it attracts orders, the Stingray II should be a very capable light tank.

SERVICE STATUS

Not yet in service; still in development.

Prototype:	1995/96
In service:	Not yet in service
Crew:	4
Armament:	Main, 105mm low recoil force 105mm rifled cannon
Combat weight:	22,600kg
Power-to-weight ratio:	24.33hp/t
Ground pressure:	Not available
Length gun forward:	9.35m
Hull length:	6.44m
Hull width:	2.7m
Height:	2.55m
Ground clearance:	0.46m
Power pack:	Detroit Diesel Model 8V-92TA of 550hp coupled to an automatic transmission
Max road speed:	71km/h
Max range (internal fuel):	450km
Fording (unprepared):	1.07m
Gradient:	60%
Side slope:	40%
Vertical obstacle:	0.84m

Futuristic looking Stingray 2 model.   *(Courtesy of the Manufacturer)*

MANUFACTURER: UNITED DEFENSE

BACKGROUND
The XM8 Armoured Gun System (AGS) is the first modern light tank designed from its onset for use by rapid reaction forces. Such a vehicle has to be easily deployable, and that means air portable. The AGS's function is to provide direct fire support for light forces where MBTs are not available.

The AGS incorporates modern technology such as modular armour, and an autoloader, yet capitalises on using proven commercially available technologies and components.

The vehicle borrows some design concepts taken from the Close Combat Vehicle-Light, a 1980s project. At present the AGS is expected to be in low rate production by 1996.

SURVIVABILITY
The AGS has extremely sophisticated and flexible armour protection. As the armour is modular, it can be replaced and upgraded when required. The basic hull and turret are made out of aluminium plus titanium plate. In addition, thin ceramic tiles bonded to Kevlar, are attached to vulnerable points. This combination, known as Level 1 Protection, offers protection against heavy

machine gun and small arms fire. Two alternate suits of modular armour, offering successively greater degrees of protection at the cost of increased weight, can be attached. Level II consists of additional aluminium, titanium and steel armour, which will defeat medium calibre cannon rounds. Level III Protection consists of advanced, passive armour boxes. This can survive the impact of infantry HEAT projectiles. A force commander can tailor protection levels according to the level of perceived threat and the type of aircraft available for the strategic lift.

The AGS is designed to withstand rough handling. Ammunition stored in the autoloader's magazine at the rear of the turret is separated from the crew by a bulkhead; blow out panels in the turret roof are in situ to reduce the effect of secondary explosions.

FIREPOWER
The tank carries the fully stabilised XM35 105mm rifled tank gun of US design. The cannon has a low recoil and a muzzle brake. The weapon is fed by an autoloader, capable of 12 shots a minute. In addition to the 21 rounds stowed in the autoloader's magazine at the left rear of the turret, nine rounds are stowed in the hull. Ammunition is standard 105mm NATO rounds. If the autoloader breaks down then the gunner can load manually.

Fire control is exceptionally sophisticated for a light tank. Components from fire control systems already in service are used. The digital computer is a modified version of that used by Challenger 2. The gunner's sight incorporates thermal imaging and laser rangefinding capabilities similar to that of the Korean Type 88 MBT.

MOBILITY
Strategic mobility is excellent. The AGS has been designed to be transported by air and even air dropped by parachute. The type of aircraft that can carry the AGS depends on its chosen level of protection. The C-130 Hercules can airdrop the AGS at Level 1 protection and carry it, but not airdrop, at Level 2. If the tank is configured at Level 3 then larger cargo aircraft, such as the C-17, are required to haul it.

At Level 1 Protection, the AGS has a high power-to-

United Defense XM8 Armoured Gun Stysystem, a pointer to the future for modular armour design.
(Courtesy of the Manufacturer)

weight ratio; its agility is impaired at higher levels of protection. The power pack – based on a US Army high mobility truck – is designed for easy access and maintenance. Suspension is torsion bar with shock absorbers. The transmission is based on that of the Bradley.

ASSESSMENT

The AGS is a very important programme. Its superior strategic mobility allows it to give direct fire support to quick intervention forces. The designers have cleverly blended state of the art technology – particularly in its armour packages – with available components. This increases availability and reduces costs.

The AGS can fight enemy MBTs, but preferably in conjunction with friendly heavy armour and other support.

SERVICE STATUS

Not yet in service. Approx. 300 are expected to enter into service with US forces and Taiwan has expressed an interest.

Prototype:	1994
In service:	Not yet in service
Crew:	3
Armament:	Main, 105mm, long recoil, rifled cannon. Secondary, coaxial 7.62 mm MG, anti-aircraft 1 x 12.7mm MG
Combat weight:	Level 1, 18,052kg. Level 2, 19,958kg. Level 3, 23,586kg
Power-to-weight ratio:	Level 1, – 30.46hp/t. Level 2, – 27.55hp/t. Level 3, – 23.31hp/t
Ground pressure:	0.63kg/cm^2 (Level 1)
Length gun forward:	9.18m
Hull length:	6.1m
Hull width:	2.69m
Height (to turret roof):	2.34m
Ground clearance:	0.41m
Power pack:	Detroit Diesel Model 6V-92A of 550hp linked to a hydromechanical transmission
Max road speed:	72km/h
Max range (internal fuel):	483km
Fording (unprepared):	1.02 m
Gradient:	60%
Side slope:	40%
Vertical obstacle:	0.81m

MANUFACTURER: TELEDYNE VEHICLE SYSTEMS

BACKGROUND

The manufacturer noted in the 1970s a potential gap in the market, for an air-transportable light tank, with an effective kinetic punch. A unique configuration with many important technological innovations resulted. The designers saved weight and reduced the vehicles silhouette, by employing an external gun pod rather than a conventional turret. An autoloader and a front mounted engine, were some of the many other interesting design concepts employed by the Expeditionary Tank.

Developed throughout the 1980s, the Expeditionary Tank has failed to take any orders. However its advanced, external gun pod, is being actively marketed for use on many contemporary MBTs.

PROTECTION

The Expeditionary Tank has a number of distinctive features that improve its survivability. Like the Israeli Merkava MBT, the Expeditionary Tank has an unusual configuration with the power pack at the front. A front mounted engine, and explosion-resistant fuel cells, act as a form of spaced armour augmenting the level of crew protection. As the gun pod is smaller and lighter than a conventional turret, it allows extra armour to be used around the crew compartment without the tank exceeding its designed weight limits. Armour consists of advanced laminates used in conjunction with steel. All ammunition is stowed below the level of the external gun pod. The general low profile and the reduced silhouette of the gun pod, help to maximise survivability.

The driver is situated to the left of the hull front, but well behind the front road wheel, thus increasing his chance of surviving a mine blast. Double-skinned belly plates, also help the tank's crew to survive mine explosions. An automatic fire detection/suppression system is fitted as standard.

FIREPOWER

A novel external gun mounting, using an autoloader and a soft-recoil 105mm rifled gun, give the vehicle impressive firepower disproportionate to its light weight. The gun is fully stabilised. The cannon can fire 10 to 12 rounds a minute. The autoloader is fed from an 8 round drum, low down in the fighting compartment. The drum itself, is replenished from a 22 round magazine in the rear of the tank. The Expeditionary Tank is relatively easy

Teledyne Vehicle Systems Expeditionary Tank/Armoured Gun System utilising a sophisticated turret. *(Courtesy of the Manufacturer)*

to bomb up with its compartmentalised, rear mounted magazine.

Fire control, sights and optics are modern and comprehensive, borrowing from equipment standard on the M60A3. A digital fire control computer, thermal imagery and laser range finding are all installed.

MOBILITY

The Expeditionary Tank has the same power train as the Bradley series IFVs. Power to weight ratio is impressive, and the Teledyne designed external, hydropneumatic suspension system, offers a good ride to complement the vehicle's agility. The drive sprocket is at the front. Prototypes have five pairs of road wheels; production models will have six. The road wheels are identical to those of the M109 self-propelled gun.

ASSESSMENT

The specific market niche that the vehicle was meant to fill, appears to have been seized by the XM8 Armoured Gun System. Nevertheless the Expeditionary tank has a comparable level of technological innovation and the project is far from dead. Its turret is being marketed as a replacement for the turrets of obsolescent MBTs, giving them a new lease of life, whilst the hull with its front mounted engine is ideal for use as the basis for an IFV or other fighting machines.

SERVICE STATUS

Prototype only.

Prototype:	1985
In service:	Not yet in service
Crew:	3
Armament:	Main, 105mm reduced recoil rifled cannon. Secondary, coaxial 1 x 7.62 mm MG, anti-aircraft 1 x 7.62 mm MG
Combat weight:	19,051kg
Power-to-weight ratio:	31.49hp/t
Ground pressure:	0.696kg/cm²
Length gun forward:	7.49m
Hull length:	6.273m
Hull width:	2.692 m
Height (to top of gun pod):	2.54m
Ground clearance:	0.482 m
Power pack:	Cummins VTA-930T V-8 turbocharged diesel of 600hp coupled to an automatic transmission
Max road speed:	70 to 80km/h
Max range (internal fuel):	482km
Fording (unprepared):	1.22 m
Gradient:	60%
Side slope:	40%
Vertical obstacle:	0.838m